MASTER MEMBER

INSTITUTE OF
VIDEOGRAPHY

Both Sides of the Movie Camera

Short Film Making Techniques

for

Directors and Actors

GU00457315

INCLUDING

**ORIGINAL SHORT SCREENPLAY CHALLENGES
TO PRODUCE, ADAPT AND WORKSHOP YOUR
NEW FOUND FILMMAKING/ACTING SKILLS**

Anthony Barnett

30130 5061 7602 2

First published 2020
by Publishing Push
The Courtyard, 30 Worthing Road, Horsham, West Sussex, England, RH12 1SL

Cover design by publishingpush.com

© by Anthony Barnett

The right of Anthony Barnett to be identified as author of this work has been
asserted by him in accordance with sections 77 and 78 of the Copyright, Designs
and Patents Act 1988.

The author gives permission for a script from the Take 1 & Take 2 section
of the book to be downloaded from the books website

www.bothsidesofthemoviecamera.film

to be used as recommended in the text of the book.

If filmed, the author must be credited as,
Screenplay by Anthony Barnett, or acknowledged as,
adapted from a script/idea (as either or may be) by Anthony Barnett

Appendices 1–4 resources may freely be downloaded from the books website.

Otherwise, all rights reserved. No part of the book may be reprinted or reproduced
or utilised in any form or by any electronic, mechanical, or other means, now known
or hereafter invented, including photocopying and recording, or in any information
storage or retrieval system, without permission in writing from the publishers.

Product or corporate names may be trademarks or registered trademarks, and are used only for identification and explanation without intent to infringe.

British Library Cataloguing-in-Publication Data
ISBN Paperback: 978-1-913704-39-1
ISBN eBook: 978-1-913704-40-7

Library of Congress Subject Headings
Vocational guidance - Film/TV/Performing Arts, Drama, Theatre, Performance Studies, Directing/Cinema Studies, Motion Picture Production, Screen Acting, Media.

Dedication

For Jacquetta who wisely did not follow her dad into
this profession after she decided that my direction of her
LAMDA exam piece at the age of six had cost her
the honour grade resulting in only a merit.

Contents

Foreword

Anthony brings something truly useful from the breadth of his experience as an actor, director, and film producer. He says "the contents of *Both Sides of the Movie Camera* is a book that I would have welcomed reading when I started out on my career. It shows how being introduced to the technical side of filmmaking for actors can alleviate the fear of the unknown allowing for the relationship between director and actor to flourish with an appreciation of each other's craft leading to a successful collaboration in bringing a screenplay to life".

There are many books that tackle one or other aspect but few, if any, that bring these crafts together in a comprehensive and practical manner. So here we have a volume that reaches out to anyone working either side of the camera. The actor's understanding of the processes on set, and conversely the Producer/Director's grasp of the actor's art, contribute to a better mutual understanding and respect that is the foundation of constructive and creative work, all in the service of the true objective – reaching an audience with a well-made film.

Anthony has written many original short screenplays in the second part of the book for actors and directors to work with that may be used as showreel material or produced as fully-fledged short films.

Whether you are new to all this or a seasoned professional there is much to learn between these covers plus 'interactive' QR links to examples and an invitation to participate and comment beyond the book via the dedicated website

www.bothsidesofthemoviecamera.film

Tony Manning
CEO/Chairman

**INSTITUTE OF
VIDEOGRAPHY**

Introduction

"I want to direct this screenplay. Having read it I can visualise exactly how I want it to be viewed. I can see how each character needs to look and speak. I'm going to be responsible for both sides of the camera - but how?"

"I've been cast in this film. I'm nervous about acting on screen. I've heard that there's a difference between that and stage acting. I want to give a screen performance - but how?"

How

to bring the director and actor an understanding of each other's craft so that they may create a movie '...giving people little tiny pieces of time...that they never forget'[1] is what the following aims to show you...

---

[1] James Stewart.

Walk before you Leap Q & A

Making a short film gives you the opportunity to gain experience...

Q. **What is experience?**

A. "Experience is simply the name we give our mistakes." Oscar Wilde

Directors:

Q. **Why make a short film?**

A. The art of how to make a film can all be learned cost effectively by embracing this genre.

Q. **Wouldn't it be better to make the full length movie that I've written?**

A. You'll need a lot of finance for that. It also, for a first attempt, will more than likely end up as 'car crash filmmaking', leaving you with a hefty overdraft and many broken promises.

What better way to avoid that nightmare than to prove to an investor or employer that their money may not be wasted, by offering them a viewing of a short film, that you have made, that shows them your potential, without showing them the many "mistakes" you may have learnt from along the way. Occasionally as Henry Ford appreciated "A mistake may turn out to be the one thing necessary to a worthwhile achievement.".

Q. **Where could I show my short film?**

A. In competitions. There are many, if you look out for them online (some referenced p. 322). They often usefully do not give a theme, but do usually stipulate a maximum length.

Q. **What would be the point of entering a film competition?**

A. Win, or come 2nd or 3rd and you have got yourself a great calling-card for employers or investors. Plus, the feedback you will get from not only the judges but the audience will be invaluable for future projects.

Q. As an unknown how can I get noticed?

A. By making a short film! Short enough to want more; long enough to impress. You want your work to be seen. By offering a busy potential employer or investor this genre your wish is more likely to be fulfilled

Actors:

Q. How can I use this guide to improve my screen acting?

A. The information here will give you a complete understanding of the mechanics of filmmaking and the requirements for you to give a screen performance. With that knowledge you will confidently perform for the camera. Use the scripts to practice your technique on camera, or to complete a showreel for casting directors.

Single Camera Q & A

Cinematographer with ARRI Cinematic Camera

Q. Why do filmmakers use only one camera?

A.

a/ Because it gives you complete control over each shot; lighting, sound, acting, mise en scene, atmosphere.

b/ One camera makes it cheaper to resource, although more expensive with time.

c/ However: use more than one for an action sequence where crashing cars or blowing up a building can only be done once. This expense is unlikely for a short film budget!

d/ A star like Robert De Niro may want their performance covered using a variety of shots "…if it's a very emotional scene, it's very hard. That's why I like to use several cameras. Otherwise I might have to get myself worked up again…"[2]

Pre-Production Q & A

Q. What is Pre-Production?

A. "Fail to prepare and you prepare to fail". The following pre-production items prior to the first day of your shoot that will need to have been prepared are…

Script – Shooting Script/Storyboard/Shot list/budget etc.

Production form examples are in the Appendix with online templates at www. bothsidesofthemoviecamera.film to be completed for the following

Budget
Casting
Crew recruitment
Actors & Crew contracts
Health & Safety (risk assessment)
Copyright
Permissions
Location Release forms
Shot List
Shooting Schedule
Hiring/Purchasing/Borrowing equipment

Q. What do I do first?

A. "To make a great film you need three things – the script, the script and the script." Now assuming you have Alfred Hitchcock's three things to hand let's first look at creating either a storyboard or a shooting script.

---

[2] CARDULLO, B. et al (1998) Playing To The Camera. Yale University Press. p.292

Q. Is creating a storyboard essential?

Storyboard by Charles Ratteray for Joss Whedon's "Buffy the Vampire Slayer"

A. No. Werner Herzog - David Cronenberg - Steven Spielberg (*Schindler's List* Best Picture Oscar) to name but a few industry titans have flown from the high wire without this industry standard safety net. That said perhaps before you venture out on the wire, learning how and why to storyboard may be a wise health and safety pre-production preparation. Just bear in mind you don't need to become a perfectionist with them. They will merely be a tool to assist you to get your virtual reality vision in through the lens of the camera to the movie screen.

Q. What if I can't draw?

A. There are many software packages that I list at the back of this book that may be used (p. 321) but the best come at a price. One cost-effective method is to take stills from films or create your own still shots possibly at the location creating 'pre-visualization' shots then placing them as a storyboard alongside the dialogue. The following shows how your storyboard could look showing camera movement in a deconstruction of a scene from *Charade* (1963) Screenplay: Peter Stone. Director: Stanley Donen.

Charade

59. INT. FUNERAL CHAPEL -- DAY

Having watched SCOBIE exit, suddenly a hand falls on her shoulder. She jumps in alarm and utters a little cry of fright.

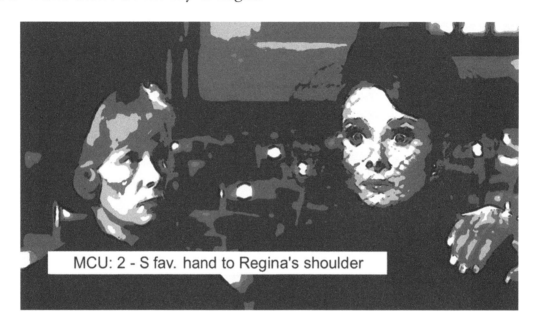

MCU: 2 - S fav. hand to Regina's shoulder

60. ANOTHER ANGLE

Featuring a funeral ATTENDANT, a cadaverous type (aren't they all) with a black cut-away coat and an over-solicitous, unctuous manner. He is eternally bent at the waist, in a sort of half bow. He offers REGGIE a letter which she takes.

MCU: tilt down - track back to 3 - S.

He offers REGGIE a letter...

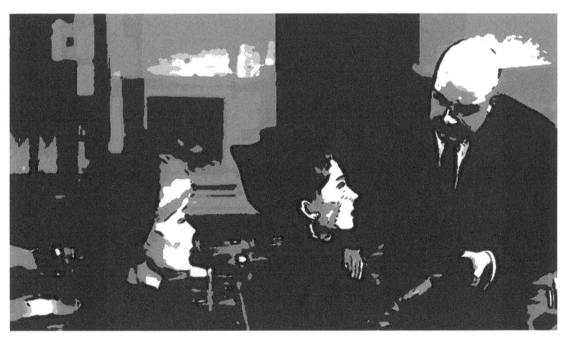

...which she takes.

REGGIE
Merci, Monsieur.

ATTENDANT
Pas du tout, madame, pardon -- pardon -- pardon.

3 - S: fav. Regina with letter

He backs off and is gone. REGGIE looks at the letter, back and front, then starts to open it.

SYLVIE
Who is it from?

REGGIE
The American Embassy.

She pulls out the letter and starts to read it.

61. INSERT -- THE LETTER

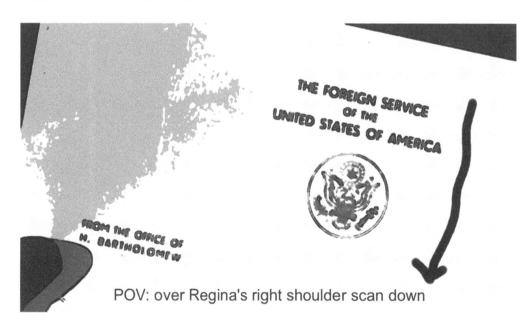

THE FOREIGN SERVICE
OF THE
UNITED STATES OF AMERICA

FROM THE OFFICE OF
H. BARTHOLOMEW

POV: over Regina's right shoulder scan down

It bears the Great Seal as a letterhead and the typed message reads:

Dear Mrs. Lampert:

Please drop by my office tomorrow at noon-thirty. I am anxious to discuss the matter of your late husband's death.

Sincerely, (signed) H. Bartholomew."

END
The scene can be viewed using the QR code here

https://archive.org/details/Charade19631280x696
Funeral Scene at 15.30 - 18.50

Q. So, to storyboard or not to storyboard?

A. It will save a lot of time if your crew and actors can instantly be presented with your visual concept of the scene. The above Charade sequence, with you as director, could now be brought to life by showing it to your crew and cast. This in a far shorter time than repeatedly having to explain and possibly being misunderstood leading to the following...

> **Director & Actor note:**
>
> 'During production most directors show signs of acute insecurity (depression - manic energy - low flashpoint - panic - irresolution). If that is not enough to puzzle crew members the director's mental state often generates superhuman energy and endurance that tests crew members to the limit'.
>
> *Raiger M (2013) Directing: Film Techniques and Aesthetics*

Shooting Script Q & A

Q. If I don't storyboard how will I know what to shoot?

A. Create a **Shooting Script** like the following. At first it may look confusing but don't panic – all will be explained.

ACTRESS FIRST TIME ON SET

FADE IN

1. INT: LIVING ROOM - DAY

We see an ACTOR and an ACTRESS

ACTOR

A	This is your first time filming? Don't worry
Master Shot	I'll explain. The camera in position **A** is t taking a Master Shot of us. **/**

ACTRESS

B	That's as if we were on the stage and
MCU	camera **A** was the audience? **/**

ACTOR

C	Yes - after that we are going to have to do
CU	this scene again. **/**

ACTRESS

B	Again? **/**
MCU	

8

ACTOR

A _____ Yes - for the camera in position **B** /
Master Shot

ACTRESS

But there is no camera in position **B**

ACTOR

It'll be the same camera moved to position **B**
C _____ for my Medium Close Up and Close Up./
MCU

ACTRESS

B _____ But camera **B** can't see me./
MCU

ACTOR

C _____ It may see the back of your head and shoulder/
MCU

ACTRESS

But we've already done the scene with the camera
being able to see both of us. Why would
A _____ it now be pointing at you? /
Master Shot

ACTOR

To provide a variety of shots for Editing. The editor will
have all of the different camera positions to choose from,
ABC _____ selecting the best to tell the story./
Quick montage of all angles and shot sizes

A _____ /
Master Shot

ACTRESS

Do I have to say the same lines all over again?

ACTOR

C   Yes - and again when the camera is moved to
MCU   position **C**./
Then it will be looking over my shoulder to you for your
Medium Close Up and Close Up

ACTRESS

A   Why don't they use three cameras? Then we could do it
Master Shot   in one take ?./

ACTOR

Ah. You'd better read the beginning of this book at Scene 1!

Both look into the lens of camera position **A** and hear...

EDITOR V.O.

Yes - and please Actors know your lines and actions backwards so that you repeat the same lines when action is called during each camera position.

DIRECTOR V.O.

I've marked this script for myself and the editor to see where I think each cut could be by the forward slash **/** and **A - Z** lettering for the crew to see the camera positions.

FADE OUT

Director note: the above lines drawn under the dialogue contain letters **A** - **B** or **C** in the left margin above the line representing camera positions with shot sizes below. The forward slash ---**/** is at the point that the camera named on the line is cut to...**confused?**

Q. **Confused and panicked – please explain?**

A. I promise you the following will make the previous *Actress First Time On Set* **shooting script** an understandable process that you may find useful to adopt for your film instead of storyboarding, or indeed you may find it useful to use a mix of both, leading to compilation of another essential item explained later the **Shot List**...

First create a

Location/Studio Floor Plan

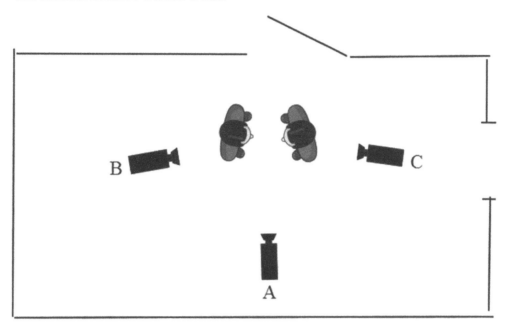

Planning single camera positions marking them **A –Z** above. You will get your 'coverage' with some of the following shot sizes of your actors as in the scene below where the cameras are positioned in the above single-camera plan

Master Shot Camera position **A**

Reverse Medium Close Up (MCU). Camera position **B** on Actor, **C** on Actress

Reverse Close Up (CU) Camera position **B** on Actor, **C** on Actress

Reverse Big Close Ups (BCU) Camera position **B** on Actor, **C** on Actress

Reverse Extreme Close Up (ECU) Camera position **B** on Man, **C** on Woman

Director and Actor note: the above has now shown you the relevance of the *Actress First Time On Set* Shooting Script mark-up with camera position letters **A – Z** and shot sizes.

You see director – no need to have panicked.

Using this process will give both Director and Actor confidence with the most complex of scenes

Technically the previous shots have been achieved by not crossing the line/ breaking the 180-degree rule.

Q. What is the 180-degree rule?

A. Ah! now you need to be patient: take your time understanding the following to avoid many frustrating times in the edit with unusable shots like these...

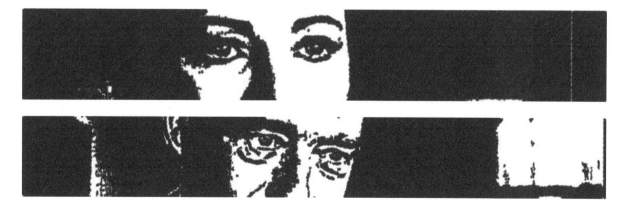

...where your actors are no longer looking at each other when you try to edit! This is because the line (180-degree rule) has been crossed when positioning camera B, as in the sketch below.

Wrong - Camera B has crossed the line!

180 Degree Rule - How not to cross the Line

How to never get it wrong:

a/ Looking at the Master Shot above, always imagine you are in the place of the camera (position **A** in the sketch above) looking at both actors. Between their heads imagine a line from the side you are filming (in this case camera position **A**). Camera positions **B** & **C** must never cross that line filming behind the actors as we see in the sketch above where camera **B** has [Camera B is guilty of having crossed the line!], causing the Actor not to be looking at the Actress when edited.

b/ The Master Shot shows the Actress screen left and the Actor screen right. All the following variety of sized reverse shots need to bear these actor positions in mind: Camera **B** focussing on the male placed screen right looking screen left; Camera **C** focussing on the female placed screen left looking screen right.

c/ By making sure the back of an actor's head in the reverse shots is placed screen right or left respectively you leave plenty of what is known as 'nose room' (space between their nose and the edge of the frame in the direction they are looking) as seen in the shots above.

d/ In the above Master Shot, the Actor is taller than the Actress; for the eye-line to be correct in all of the reverse shots the camera has been set at each actor's respective height looking either up or down from their viewpoint.

Q. **What if the standing talent is too tall to place the camera at their height for a reverse shot?**

A. Place the shot at a comfortable angle below the tall talent's height, making sure the talent in the reverse shot is keeping their eyeline looking towards the tall talent's eyes above the screen frame.

Q. **what do I do with the 180 degree rule if a character changes position on screen?**

A.

a/ In the following Master Shot from *Farewell To Arms* (1932) starring Gary Cooper

we see from camera position 'A' the following Master Shot.

Then the actor standing on the right crosses behind Gary Cooper sitting as seen below

Where we see the moving actor now on left of screen as below

The line of action has not changed. The standing actor has; because the actor was seen crossing behind the sitting actor the viewer will not be confused with the following change in the reverse shots. Camera position **C** focussing on the standing actor will now be a MCU with his head left of screen looking (down) towards screen right. The sitting actor with the camera in position **B** focussing on his MCU will now have his head screen right looking (up) towards screen left – with (remember) plenty of 'nose room' for both.

If we did not see the standing actor crossing behind the sitting actor right to left, the subsequent reverse shot would not edit together. Always remember to ask yourself, what position the actors are in, after you have movement in a Master Shot and make sure you show the movement happening in a Master Shot.

b/ The line of action can be crossed/changed as long as movement is shown to the viewer (geographically). View the scene at following QR *Farewell To Arms* at 56.57

https://youtu.be/mBao7an_crY

Here is a more complex sequence from Frank Capra's *It's a Wonderful Life* (1947) starring James Stewart and Donna Reed

1. Master Shot

2. Donna moves off   3. James picks up a stone

4. Donna returns   5. Line crossed with view of derelict house

6. Making a wish before throwing stone   7. Single shot of derelict house

8. About to throw stone window   9. James throws stone smashing window

10. Man on balcony hears glass smash   11. Donna & James flirt

12. Donna & James continue to flirt   13. Donna looks with idea to make a wish

14. Donna throws stone shattering glass

15. Both look with glee at result

16. Off again flirting down the street

17. Man on balcony still watching

18. James passes behind Donna

19. James now is left of screen

20. Man can be seen on balcony behind

21. Man's eyeline to where they have moved to

22. James signals the moon
23. Eyes have got us looking at moon

24. Camera seeing in 'Depth' Man behind
25. Man light heartedly yells for him to kiss her

26. Man's POV of them both

This scene works because we are always informed as a viewer, where the actors look, taking us backwards and forwards to new lines of action and the POV from the Man on the balcony whose house is on the same side of the street as they are. The scene can be viewed here

It's A Wonderful Life

https://youtu.be/Xa0v8hJk8aY

How to keep the 180-Degree rule line of action with more than 2 characters

Q. When there are more than 2 characters in conversation in a shot, how can I make sure that, in their individual reverses, they are looking as if they are talking to each other?

A. With difficulty! The following type of planned single-camera positions **A - E** below is one way...

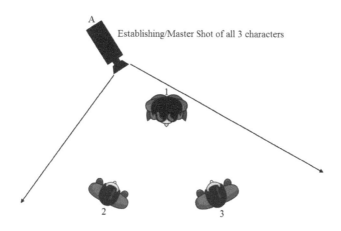

Establishing/Master Shot of all 3 characters

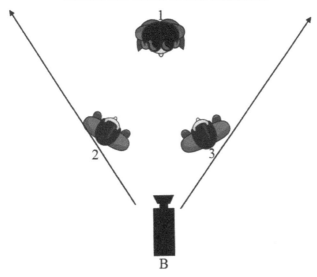

Master Shot No:2 of all 3 characters

Character 1 (placed centre screen) looking left & right of camera to 2 & 3

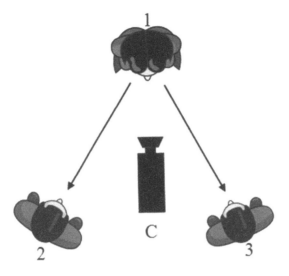

Character 2 (placed centre screen) looking left of Camera to character 1 and right to character 2

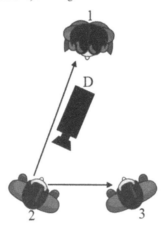

Character 3 (placed centre screen) looking right past camera to 1 and left to 2

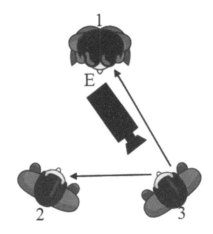

Director and Actor note: It is vital to make sure that actors do not jump out at the viewer by 'spiking' the camera lens (looking into the lens **BREAKING** the **FOURTH WALL**). This is something that can happen fleetingly, unintentionally by the performer, surprising everyone in the edit.

N.B. This convention can be broken deliberately with a leading character sharing a touch of dramatic irony with the viewer - in theatre this is known as an 'aside'. One of the earliest examples of **BREAKING** the **FOURTH WALL** in film can be seen in Agatha Christie's *And Then There Were None* (1945)

https://youtu.be/HrkQMivgAGo
6.25 - 7.15

Filmmakers Woody Allen *Annie Hall* (1977) Spike Lee *Do The Right Thing* (1989) - and many others – have used this device since.

<u>Plus:</u> if done 'subtly' by a leading character under their director's instruction it can be very affective, if it is just a **momentary knowing glance** to us the audience in front of another character who doesn't see it. BBC's *Fleabag* with Waller-Bridge's asides is the perfectly performed and directed example.

The following is an alternative 3 shot single camera A-Z set up...

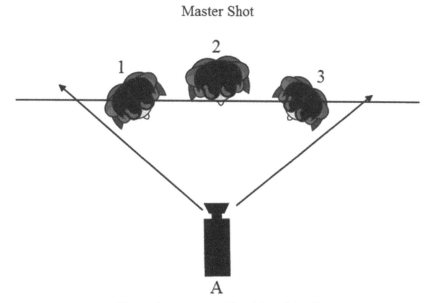

Master Shot

Keep the camera this side of the line

2 shot of 1 & 2 talking to each other & to 3

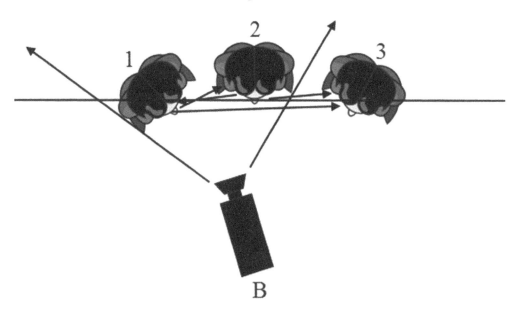

Keep the camera this side of the line

Single Shot Character 3 (placed screen right) looking left with 'nose room' to 1 & 2

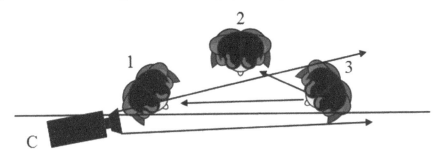

Keep the camera this side of the line

Here you could cut back to the Master Shot

The above camera position **C** could not cut to a 2 shot of 2 & 3 because it would mean that from camera position **B** with the 2 shot on 1 & 2, character 2 would jump from Right to Left of screen if you cut between the two.

With the above single shot of character 3 and a cut back to the Master Shot

Character 2 (placed centre screen) able to look left & right to 1 & 3

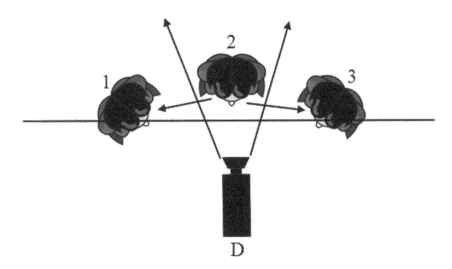

Keep the camera this side of the line

You can now introduce more single shots like the following...

Character 1 (placed left of screen) plenty of 'nose room' to look right

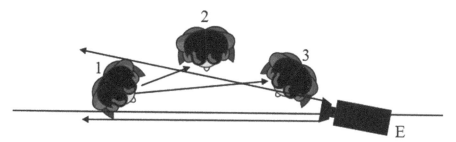

Keep the camera this side of the line

These are the basics that you need to know for crossing the line, eye-lines and not breaking the 180-degree rule. With larger casts the principles are the same only more complex. With knowledge of the above, you will now be able to work it out, with caution.

Director note: there are many examples in films when the line of action is unintentionally crossed - *The Room* (2003) being one example. Unintentionally being the operative word because as in Lars von *Trier's Dogville* (2003) it is very intentional.

Its disorientating effect is used by filmmakers for a documentary feel or to deliberately confuse the viewer or show characters experiencing confusion. Make sure if it happens in your films - it is intentional!

Shooting Script

Q. What is a Shooting Script?

A. Each location scene heading needs to be numbered in the script or storyboard as can be seen with the *Charade* script in this book. The numbering is from 1 to 101 and probably upwards enumerating as many separate scenes as there are.

Q. Why?

A. Location location location - you only want to go to and set up once at each location. The first day of a shoot may be filming in a character's house. Throughout the storyline the character may be seen in their house in Shot List scenes 4, 20, 32, 51 and 120 (being perhaps the final scene when they pass away in the film).

Every location throughout the film needs to have all the scenes in the Shooting Script, relevant to each location, filmed before moving on to the next.

> **Actor note:** you will hear many times actors saying that they shot their death bed scene on the first day of a shoot even though their character survives most of the film. Above is the reason why. Make sure you are prepared enough for this higgledy piggledy assault on your senses for it not to affect your performance. You don't want your performance to die before you have started!

Shot List

Q. What is a shot list?

A. For each location in the Shooting Script a list of the shots for each scene (Master Shot - MCU - CU etc) to be filmed needs to have been written up so that nothing will be missed. This then will be available with the Shooting Schedule. See the example Shot List form in Appendix 1 and use the template available at www.bothsidesofthemoviecamera.film

Splitting a script into eighths – creating a Script breakdown Sheet/Production Board for Budgeting and Shooting Schedule

Q. What are all these documents for?

A. They instruct on budgeting requirements and the time needed for each shoot day. It instructs where (Location) - when (Day) what (Scene) what (technical equipment) what (crew, cast etc.) what (props, costume, makeup) everything relating to the avoidance of a wasted day (see contingency plan in glossary). Splitting a script into eighths for budgeting and scheduling is explained in Appendix 2 with templates for all other requirement at www.bothsidesofthemoviecamera.film

Filming Q & A

Call to Action

Q. What are the correct commands to "Action"?

A. **Director:** "silence on set" – "Mobile Phones Off" – "Lights?" – "Sound?" – "Camera?" – "Slate" – "Action" ...."Cut"

The Slate/Clapper Board only needs to be called for if you have one. (there is an etiquette for slating a scene that I have included in Appendix 3). Each question above requires a "Yes or No". If "No" get the problem fixed and go again.

Do not get lazy with these commands. Always use them to avoid confusion.

Director and Actor note:

a/ shoot the Master Shot first then from separate camera position with the actors performing it each time from start to finish (BCU & ECU optional).

b/ it is possible to shoot a single actor reverse without the other actor/s being there. As long as they are looking at where the other characters should be and at the correct eyeline and height.

Why might you do this? – Why might it work better?

If the other actor/s are not available. Get someone to read the lines off camera for the on-camera actor to speak and react. This can lead to a better performance for the on-camera actor, because they do not feel obliged to please their fellow actor, it frees them to perhaps take risks with their performance uninhibitedly.

c/ get your actors to be doing something before you say 'Action' and do not say 'Cut' too soon. Allow some time after the end of a shot – then say 'Cut'. With both before and after movement/action all will be easier to edit.

N.B. Master Shot: although this is important - do not sacrifice time on it for all of the other combination of shots that you have planned. Shots that are vital for the pace, story and emotion of each scene. Without them you will have a piece of theatre with the camera in Master Shot watching. Your Editor will not be pleased - your actors will not be pleased - your audience will be bored.

Putting the 'Busy' into Business...
or a 'Continuity' nightmare?

Q. What is 'Business'?

A. There are two types of business. One is plot business where props like the letter in the storyboard charade scene in Scene 1 are a necessity. Then there is the director's or actor's invented character business where imagination can transform a scene creating reality and movement.

Q. What does a 'Busy' scene look like?

A. The following deconstruction once again from Charade is a fine example of a 'Busy' scene that has both types of business but no 'continuity' errors although there are some that can be noted at other parts of the movie at the following link https://www.moviemistakes.com/film4230

Here - using the final script you will also see how changes are made at the last minute on set/location allowing for the inspiration that can lead to what director Spike Lee has acknowledged as 'A lot of times you get credit for stuff in your movie that you didn't intend to be there.'. (note the Shooting Script numbering for when you come to do a **Shot List**)

68. INT. ESTABLISHING SHOT - AMERICAN EMBASSY - DAY

Establishing Shot

69. INT. EMBASSY LIFT -- DAY

As REGGIE leaves the elevator two young DIPLOMATIC TYPES step in, immersed in conversation.

MCU: holding letter up into shot

The elevator door closes on them. REGGIE reacts to this and starts down the hall, finally stopping at the door.

70. MED. SHOT -- DOOR

It is marked "307-A H. BARTHOLOMEW." REGGIE checks the letter, then opens the door.

MS: Regina

71. INT. BARTHOLOMEW'S OUTER OFFICE -- DAY

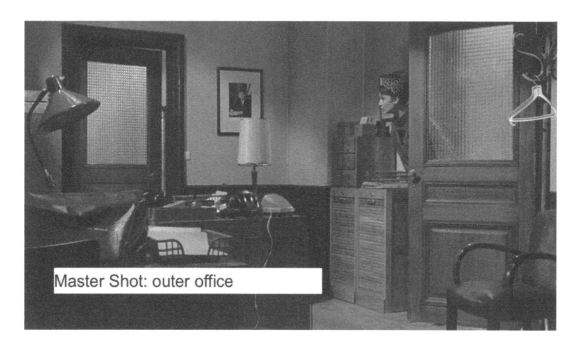

Master Shot: outer office

The office is empty, the typewriter on the secretary's desk is covered with its plastic shroud. REGGIE enters, looks for somebody, notices that the door to the private office is slightly ajar.

REGGIE
(tentatively)

CU: Single Shot

Hello -- ?
(there is no answer)
Hello?

BARTHOLOMEW'S VOICE
(o.s.)
(from the private office)
Is there anything wrong, Miss Tompkins?

REGGIE
Uh -- Miss Tompkins isn't here.

BARTHOLOMEW comes to the door and looks in. He is a pale grey-haired man who looks, on first examination, older than his forty-odd years. Sickly would be the word that describes him best -- pallid, consumptive-looking. He wears heavy tortoise-framed glasses which fall down his nose and cause him to push them back in place every so often with a quick automatic motion.

Actor note: above is an example of how the previous description of the character by Peter Stone the screenwriter and the final casting by the director Stanley Donen can be changed - in this case to the great comedic screen actor Walter Matthau's availability at the time! So if you believe you can do a part but do not fit the description - go and convince them.

Master Shot: Bartholomew & Regina

BARTHOLOMEW
I'm sorry -- my secretary must have gone
to lunch. You are -- ?

REGGIE
Mrs. Lampert -- Mrs. Charles Lampert.

BARTHOLOMEW
(looking at his watch)
Come in, Mrs. Lampert. You're quite late.

MCU: fav Bartholamew

He motions for her to enter, standing aside to let her do so.

72. INT. BARTHOLOMEW'S PRIVATE OFFICE -- DAY

A small cubicle -- there is a silver-framed photo of three kids on the desk. BARTHOLOMEW indicates a chair, then goes behind his desk and sits. A can of lighter fluid stands open on the desk and a crumpled hankie beside it.

Master Shot: private office

BARTHOLOMEW
Excuse me for a moment, Mrs. Lampert -
it's a stubborn little devil.

> **Director note:** a far better alternative by the director to the screenwriter's placement of props referred to above has been found with the added benefit of mirror shots.

Character business

He works at a stain on his necktie with lighter fluid and hankie.

BARTHOLOMEW
Dry cleaning wise, things are all fouled up.
I had a good man - an excellent man on
the Rue Ponthieu, but H.Q. asked us to use the place here in the building to
ease the gold outflow.
REGGIE
Mr. Bartholomew -- are you sure you know who I am?

BARTHOLOMEW
(looking up)
Charles Lampert's widow -- yes?

MCU: added effect of mirror

(going back to the tie)
Last time I sent out a tie only the spot came back.
He looks up at her, laughs silently,
then goes back to his tie.
Voila! As they say.

He puts away the lighter fluid in a desk drawer, smells the hankie, passes on it, then sticks it in his pocket.

MCU: move out of frame that will change the line of action

Master Shot: showing another part of the office

He opens another drawer and pulls out various sandwiches wrapped in waxpaper, a salt and pepper shaker, a tube of mustard, a bottle of red wine and two Dixie cups.

BARTHOLOMEW
Have some, please. I've got . . . (checking)
. . . liverwurst -- liverwurst -- chicken and -- liverwurst.

REGGIE
No thanks.

He uncorks the wine, fills a cup and begins eating.

BARTHOLOMEW
Do you know what C.I.A. is, Mrs. Lampert?

REGGIE
I don't suppose it's an airline, is it?

BARTHOLOMEW
Central Intelligence Agency -- C.I.A.

REGGIE
(surprised)
You mean spies and things like that?

BARTHOLOMEW
Only we call them agents.

REGGIE
We? You mean you're --?

BARTHOLOMEW
Someone has to do it, Mrs. Lampert --

37

REGGIE
I'm sorry, it's just that I didn't think that
you people were supposed to admit --

BARTHOLOMEW
I'm not an agent, Mrs. Lampert -- I'm an administrator --
a desk jockey -- trying to run a bureau of overworked men with
under-allocated funds. Congress seems to think that all a spy needs --

REGGIE
Agent.

BARTHOLOMEW
Yes -- That all he needs is a code book and a
cyanide pill and he's in business.

REGGIE
What's all this got to do with me, Mr. Bartholomew?

BARTHOLOMEW
(his mouth full)
Your husband was wanted by the U. S. government.

REGGIE
(a pause)
May I have a sandwich, please?

He hands her a sandwich and fills a wine-cup for her.

BARTHOLOMEW
To be more specific, he was wanted by this agency.

REGGIE
(eating)
So that was it.

BARTHOLOMEW
Yes. We knew him, of course, by his real name.

REGGIE
(almost choking)
His -- real -- ?

BARTHOLOMEW
Voss -- Charles Voss. All right, Mrs. Voss --
-- I'd like you
to look at this photograph, please

(taking a photo from his desk)

-- by the way, you saw this one, didn't you?

(indicating the kids on the desk)

Scott, Cathy, and Ham, Jr.

REGGIE
Very sweet.

BARTHOLOMEW
Aren't they? Now look at this one, Mrs. Voss, and --

REGGIE
Stop calling me that! Lampert's the name on
the marriage license.

BARTHOLOMEW
Yes -- and tell me if you recognize anyone.
Just a moment. Have a good look.

He reaches back into the drawer and pulls out a glass which he gives her.

73. CLOSE SHOT -- PHOTO

FOUR MEN, all in army uniform, sitting behind a table. The glass is held over the first, magnifying the face.

POV: with magnifying glass

74. CLOSER SHOT -- PHOTO

It's a photo of a young CHARLES LAMPERT.

REGGIE'S VOICE (o.s.)
It's Charles! Very good.

BARTHOLOMEW'S VOICE (o.s.)

Very good.

REGGIE'S VOICE (o.s.)
He looks so young -- when was this taken?

BARTHOLOMEW'S VOICE (o.s.)
1944. The next face, please.

The glass and CAMERA move to the next man -- a young TEX.

REGGIE'S VOICE (o.s.)
It's the man who came to the funeral yesterday --

BARTHOLOM
Does the name Tex Penthollow mean anything to you?

Director note: the scene continues with all of the characters being looked at in the photo and spoken about. In line with the comedy thriller genre a pleasing 'ping' sound effect is used at each magnified character with a zoom in magnifying them. This 'ping' sound effect is used elsewhere in the film at points of significance for the plot.

N.B. Dramatic licence has been used here with BARTHOLOMEW in the scene as it has been shot. Unless looking over her shoulder he would not know which character REGINA is looking at. As scripted he would have been out of shot (o.s) with us the audience assuming he was looking at the same shot as us.

75. MED. SHOT -- REGGIE AND BARTHOLOME

BARTHOLOMEW
(a pause, regarding her)
Mrs. Lampert, I'm afraid you're in a great
deal of danger.

REGGIE
Danger? Why should I be in any danger?

BARTHOLOMEW
You're Charles Voss's wife -- now that he's dead
you're their only lead.

REGGIE
Mr. Bartholomew -- if you're trying to
frighten me you're doing a really first rate job!
(she takes another sandwich).

BARTHOLOMEW
Please, do what we ask, Mrs. Lampert --
it's your only chance.

REGGIE
(eating)
Gladly, only I don't know what you want!
You haven't told me what

Continuity nightmare: eating more sandwiches

BARTHOLOMEW
Oh, haven't I? The money -- Mrs. Lampert --
the money. The $250,000 Charles Voss
received from the auction. Those three men want it, too --
they want it very badly.

REGGIE
But it's Charles's money, not theirs.

BARTHOLOMEW
(laughing)
Oh, Mrs. Lampert! I'd love to see you try
and convince them of that!
(drying his eyes)
Oh, dear

REGGIE
Then whose is it? His or theirs?

BARTHOLOMEW
Ours.

REGGIE
(she looks at him for a moment)
Oh, I see.

BARTHOLOMEW
And I'm afraid we want it back.

REGGIE
But I don't have it.

BARTHOLOMEW
That's impossible. You're the only one
who could have it.

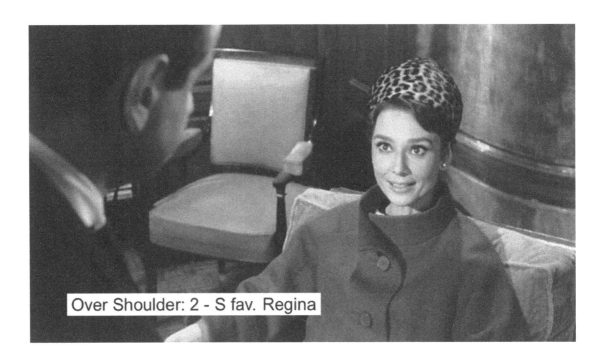

Over Shoulder: 2 - S fav. Regina

REGGIE
I'm sorry it's impossible. It's the truth.

BARTHOLOMEW
(is silent for a moment, thinking.)
I believe you.

REGGIE
Thanks very much.

BARTHOLOMEW
Oh, you've got the money all right --
you just don't know you've got it.

REGGIE
Mr. Bartholomew -- if I had a quarter
of a million dollars, believe me, I'd know it.

BARTHOLOMEW
Nevertheless, Mrs Lampert -- you've got it.

REGGIE
You mean it's just lying around someplace --
all that cash?

BARTHOLOMEW
Or a safe deposit key, a certified check,
a baggage claim -- you look for it, Mrs. Lampert --
I'm quite sure you'll find it.

Over Shoulder: 2 - S fav. Bartholomew

REGGIE
But --

BARTHOLOMEW
Look for it, Mrs. Lampert -- look just as hard

Back to behind desk with sandwich

and as fast as you can. You may not have
a great deal of time. Those men know you
have it just as surely as we do.
You won't be safe until the money's in our hands.
Is that clear?

REGGIE nods.

He writes something on a pad of paper and tears it off.

handing it to her.

BARTHOLOMEW
Here's where you're to call me -- day or night.
It's a direct line to both my office

Actor note: here he lets out a hearty belch as well he may because throughout the scene he has been eating and talking with a mouthful of sandwich and swilling down wine. Great character business.

N.B. Eating - Take a look on YouTube at any episode of the comedy Big Bang Theory whose characters are always meeting when they are eating. Notice how little they actually eat because a/ it's not easy speaking and eating b/ continuity problems would be inevitable.

A trick of the trade worth noting.

---

and my apartment.
Don't lose it, Mrs. Lampert -- and
please don't tell anyone about coming to see me.
It could prove fatal for them as well as yourself.

Back to having some wine

REGGIE
Wait a minute -- you think those three
men killed Charles, don't you?

MCU: Single Shot

BARTHOLOMEW
We've no proof, of course, but we
rather think so, yes.

REGGIE
Well, there you are! Charles had the money
with him -- so whoever killed him has it -- they have it!

BARTHOLOMEW
(shakes his head.)

REGGIE
Why not?

BARTHOLOMEW
(grimly)
Because they're still here.

REGGIE Oh.

BARTHOLOMEW
Like I said, Mrs Lampert -- I'm afraid
you're in a great deal of danger.

Remember what happened to Charles.

REGGIE takes the last sandwich and begins eating furiously.

Director note: the scene ends on two Close Ups, the final one on REGINA with the sound track of the Punch and Judy fairground music brilliantly coming in to transition to the next scene. Known as a 'J' cut. More on transitions can be found in Scene 5, Editing.

You may now like to view the scene at this QR

Charade

https://archive.org/details/Charade19631280x696
American Embassy 18.50 - 25.11

> **Actor note:** vocal levels from both actors are conversational (not theatrical). This is achieved by being aware of where the boom mic is. In the single shots it will be about a foot above your head. You only need to project to it - not to the actor sitting at a distance from you. This will mean you will be speaking quieter than normal - the pitfall with that is that speaking quietly we tend to speak slower - be aware of this making sure you keep the pace in your delivery as if you were speaking louder.
>
> Keeping the vocal level down will allow your face to be that much more relaxed allowing the camera to pick up every nuance of thought leading to a great screen performance. However – **DO NOT MUMBLE!**

Following are the previous scenes 'camera setups/positions'

INT. BARTHOLOMEW'S OUTER OFFICE -- DAY

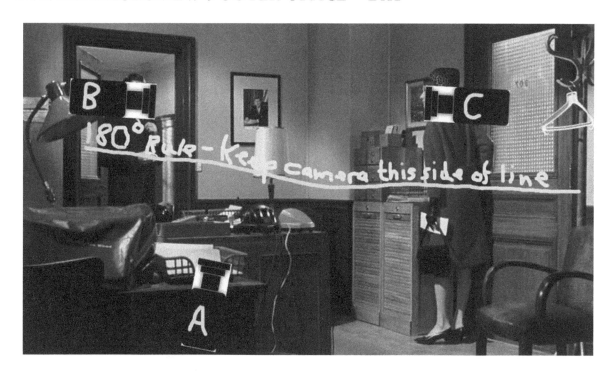

INT. BARTHOLOMEW'S PRIVATE OFFICE -- DAY

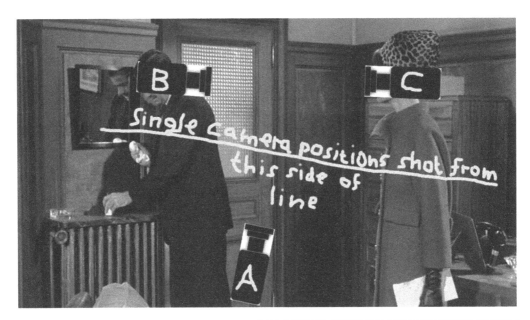

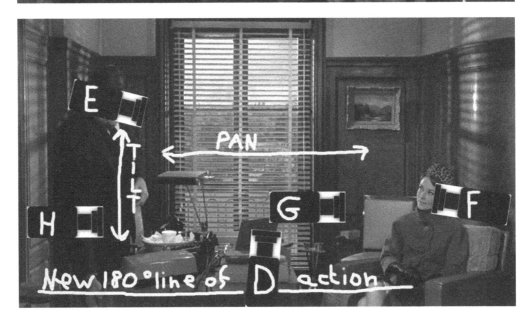

Coverage

Q. **Why are there so many different camera setups/positions?**

A. Coverage. Watching the above scenes the director Stanley Donen provides us with a master class in creating movement in what could have been a pedestrian example of a plot filled information point in the screenplay. The 8 camera positions allow for the dialogue to be delivered observing each character and their reactions providing thorough 'coverage' for the editor Jim Clark to tell the story.

> **Director note:** never rush and skimp on 'coverage'. Without it you'll have an amateur film.

Q. **It looks confusing. How would the previous scenes have been filmed?**

A. From each camera position that the cinematographer Charles Lang setup, the actors would have been directed to play the scene, take after take, repeating word for word - action for action: it would have been recorded **first** with the **Master Shot** as if watching a piece of proscenium arch theatre. The single camera positions for the Master Shots were **A** for the Outer Office scene and **A & D** for the Private Office scene.

Q. **When being filmed in a single shot what does the off-camera actor do?**

A. Eyeline: it is vital that the camera knows who the on-camera actor is talking to. (They will either be looking screen right or screen left). The off-camera actor is beside the camera giving their lines from the position the actor on camera needs to be talking to.

> **Actor & Director note:** it does not necessarily have to be the fellow actor in the scene. It could be a crew member reading the off-camera lines giving the eyeline. Surprisingly this can lead to a better performance from the single shot on camera actor due to them having the freedom to not be distracted by feeling they need to give a performance to compliment the other actor. Thus, they may feel freer to take risks as mentioned previously but worth repeating for all directors reading this.
>
> **Example:** Walter Matthau as Bartholomew in his single shots talking with his mouth full and belching... would he have felt so free to do that in front of the elegant star Audrey Hepburn as Regina if she had been the other side of the camera?

Q. How can a director maximise coverage?

A. Instinct – does the shot look right, feel right, for the story you are filming? Try high angle, low angle, panning, tilting, tracking, big close up, extreme close up shots etc.

Director note: A great classic example of 'Coverage' and 'instinct' can be seen in the famous Hitchcock *Psycho* shower scene.

'...there are 78 separate pieces of film in 45 seconds...' (Hitchcock). There are different camera positions using a variety of techniques which include in addition to locked off camera positions, panning, tilting, tracking, flash cutting (a shot that lasts for less than a second) and jump cuts.

Saul Bass the great American Graphic Designer storyboarded the scene for Hitchcock stating on film '...it went precisely as I laid it out'. This shows how important collaboration is in filmmaking between director and all concerned right down to the famous 'drain - eye' **match cut** shot that lasts 47 seconds. Hitchcock explained what he imagined allowing Bass to be creative with the storyboard submitting 48 sketches.

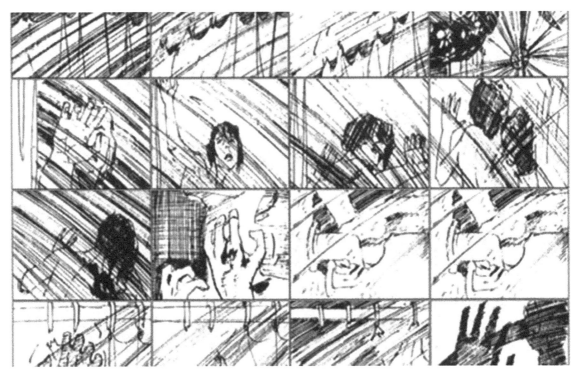

Photo courtesy of filmmakeriq

Controversially, some have implied that this iconic scene, so relevant to Hitchcock's auteur, was wholly conceived and directed by Bass.

With your Short Film allow yourself plenty of time to film plenty of creative shots and if appropriate with movement. You will then have complete control over the atmosphere you create.

Be warned: if you 'Film in haste, you will repent for ever'. The *Psycho* Shower scene took 7 days to film with early starts and late finishes each day. Take a look at it here...

Psycho

https://youtu.be/wQJJYCAH-Ww

Bad Camera Positions

Q. **Are there any bad camera positions?**

A. Yes. Looking at this illustration

45 degree plus camera position rule

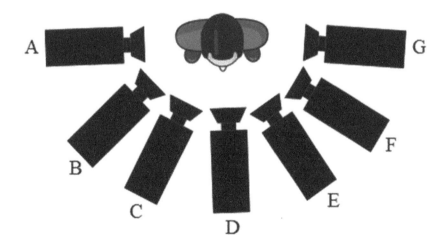

It is not advisable to place a camera less than 45 degrees from a first camera position when wanting another shot. Why? It will look messy rather like an unintentional jump cut. Shooting **A & D** would be acceptable but <u>not</u> **A** & either **B** or **C**. Likewise, **C & F** would be acceptable but <u>not</u> **C** & either **D** or **E**.

Director note: Rule of Thirds a/ keep eyes on or above the top third line of the frame b/ the major focus of action in the top third in Establishing Shots, Long Shots, Action Shots etc.

c/ in the West we read left to right. Bear in mind that because of that our eyes are drawn towards the right. This means any action on the right of screen will be in a stronger position to gain your audience's attention.

N.B. your creative instinct will on occasion demand the rule to be broken. It is to be, after all, your version of vision.

Continuity

Q. What is 'Continuity'?

A. Filmmaking is generally a single-camera activity, as you can now appreciate. With scenes being shot from several different 'single-camera setups/positions' over and over again 'continuity' is the need to have the same action with a prop or look of a hairstyle or costume repeated on the same line or moment each time the camera is shooting from a different angle on the subject. Movie Mistakes www.moviemistakes.com is a fun place to see how often an editor's 'continuity' nightmare is unavoidable given the need to use a shot.

Example: In Frank Capra's *It's a Wonderful Life* (DVD. 01.14.30 to 01.14.34) we see James Stewart enter with a Xmas Wreath on his right arm

1. He starts to take the wreath off

2. He throws the wreath on the table behind

3. No wreath on arm

4. Wreath on table between woman & man

5. Wreath on arm for remainder of conversation. We have seen the man move behind to right.

Q. How can 'continuity' errors be avoided?

A. On set you can rewind the footage and look. Not popular being too time-consuming "time is money!" Allocate someone to do the job with the title of **Script Supervisor** whose role will cover

- supervising the script to make sure the dialogue is being delivered as written by the screenwriter (taking notes of any alterations agreed on set)
- Continuity within a Scene: Matching Action

- Continuity between scenes: Progressive Action
- Technical adviser for the Grammar of Filmmaking
  (making sure the line of action is correct)

> **Actor note:** actors can help by **marking** their scripts to do something on a certain word or moment. i.e. sip a drink in a certain hand, holding it in a certain way on a certain word.

MEN

FADE IN:

INT. WINE BAR. DAY

Girl chat. Female characters A & B sit at a table. Wine
bottle between them and drinking from glasses. *[handwritten: 'B' hold glass left hand drinking]*

                    A
Why do some men claim to be sexual
athletes?

                    B
Because they always come first!
    (Both laugh) *[handwritten: put glass down - top up from bottle left hand]*

                    A
Oh you are funny...Do you ever talk to
him when you're...you Know
    (indicates making love)

                    B
Only if he telephones! *[handwritten: pick up mobile right hand - wave about - put back on table]*
    (Once again both roar with tipsy
    laughter)

                    A *[handwritten: sipping glass left hand]*
We...we...love em really...Hey...mine
walked 3 miles the other day in the
rain because the car had broken down
in the middle of nowhere and neither
of us had our phones on us.

                    B
Yeah... Well that's what they are
designed for

                    A
Yeah ...and when he came back dripping
wet I said 'what took you so long'.

                    B & A
That's what we're designed for! *[handwritten: clinking glass with 'A']*
    (Both laugh hysterically)

FADE OUT.

61

Actor note: learning your script having planned certain actions on certain words or moments when performing the same scene from different angles over and over again will win you an Oscar from directors and editors! Also, the Continuity Supervisor will love the actor who points out the drink had already been drunk. Actors love to be loved. If you are going to be that actor, make sure it's you who is loved not loathed. Yes – and hired for more parts.

N.B. Rehearsals - in film there are none! - or very rarely. At the British National Theatre, you might get 3 months to examine every nuance of the text each day followed by a year of performances to perfect your character.

For film make sure you learn your lines - rehearse and direct yourself - **before** you arrive on a set surrounded by a strange crew ready for the call of 'Action'.

POV Shots

Do not forget Point Of View shots (POV). If a character is writing as in *Psycho*

The audience wants to see what is being written from their POV, as indeed we can in the following shot, where for 3 seconds we see her bank statement and what she is writing in her note book.

This POV shot is in many of the films you will watch. However because it is only there for a few seconds, new filmmakers often miss its inclusion. It is almost subliminal – in fact I call it the '**subliminal** shot' - **don't fail to get it!** Technically it is also known as **The Subjective Camera Angle**. It needs to be shot over the shoulder nearest to the Master Shot camera position side, avoiding crossing the line (in the above POV it is over her right shoulder).

Cutaway Shots/B Roll

Do not forget: Cutaways - also known as 'B' Roll is footage that you need to 'Cutaway' to ...

as perhaps a character mentions something such as 'where did I leave my keys?'. We see in a **Cutaway** where they are but the cut back to the character shows them still looking.

or

a **Cutaway** could be anything in the background that would add relevance to a scene. The weather changing for instance - rain dripping down the window-pane etc.

Director note: Cutaways need to be given the same production values as every other part of your film with attention to lighting and sound. They are vital for assembling your film in the edit to tell the story.

Zooming

Q. When should the camera Zoom in and out of shot?

A. Never? Unless you are making a music video, or you want to make your viewer feel uncomfortable, using it as an effect as part of the story by design (see director note below).

Q. Why?

A. Because our eyes do not zoom: such a visual would make us too aware of the camera's movement: the perspective of walls etc., will close in on the image.

Dolly on a track is the answer, keeping the perspective as our eyes see it.

Director note: however there is the **Vertigo Effect** also known as the **Contra Zoom** or **Dolly Zoom.** The camera is tracked backwards as the lens is **zoomed in** on an object or person/s. The perspective (surroundings) change while the focus of interest remain static. **Examples:** *Vertigo* (1958) Jaws (1975) *Goodfellas* (1990)

Dolly Zoom - Jaws

https://youtu.be/glF3BrFu8Ls

Steadicam

Q. When should I use a Steadicam?

A.

a/ Never? In narrative screenplays when there is no rushed action. Using a Steadicam, especially when the camera cuts to a single shot of a character, we become aware of the camera operator's nervous control as the filmed content sways inside our rigid flat screens as we view. Unforgivable, regrettably too often seen. Being distracted away from the story by unnecessary camera movement should be the good director's concern, noticed and remedied during the shoot. Insist on the camera being on a Tripod (Legs/Sticks: industry terms).

b/ Yes – when action is being filmed, fast walking, running, subjective action shots (POV's) etc. Example *Goodfellas* (1990) following a couple for 2.27 seconds with an uncut shot from their car across the street into the back entrance of the Copacabana Nightclub through the kitchens to be seated in the club restaurant.

and then there's

Das Boot (1981) a German World War II Wolfgang Peterson directed U-boat submarine movie with cinematographer Jost Vacano's 35mm Arriflex adapted hand held design to create a confined claustrophobic atmosphere.

Schindler's List (1993) 40% hand held to give a documentary feel.

Birdman (2014) where the entire film is shot with steadicam and hand held, cut to give the impression of one long take for its 1Hr.59.mins. The longest take was 15 minutes with the average take being 10 minutes.

1917 (2019) Entire film shot with Arri Camera/Arri steadicam.

Director note: Hitchcock's *Rope* (1948) was edited to give the impression of one long take without the benefit of a steadicam.

It was not until 1975 when cinematographer Garrett Brown invented the Steadicam that the camera had such freedom to move. It was first used in a biopic *Bound for Glory* (1976) but really got noticed in Sylvester Stallone's *Rocky* (1976) where Garrett Brown filmed Stallone running through Philadelphia's streets and up the steps of the Philadelphia Museum of Art. It can be viewed here

Rocky

https://youtu.be/a3SVcuMTXyQ

N.B. a good quality steadicam with a highly skilled and experienced operator is the only way to succeed with this type of shot. I recommend that if you decide for your film that you need this particular style hire the best apparatus. Cheap buyable solutions are available but produce results little better than a hand-held shot - the very reason Garrett Brown invented his ergonomic steadicam to avoid.

The Takeaway: if you allow the camera work to become intrusively noticeable, you will irritate your audience causing the telling of your story to suffer.

Film vs Theatre

Q. What is the main difference a director needs to be aware of between theatre and film?

A.

a/ The camera lens has its audience viewing in depth not, as in the theatre, width. A wide-angle lens can be used but it will distort if too close.

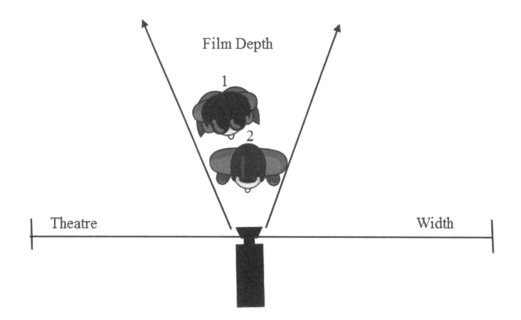

This needs to be borne in mind when directing (blocking) more than one person in the shot. The above sketch has two characters talking to each other with the viewer being able to see both of their faces. Possibly unnatural in real life, but on camera a scene played this way depending on the content would work.

Character 1
Am I pretty or ugly?

Character 2
You're both.

Character 1
What do you mean?

Character 2
You're pretty ugly.

Director and Actor note: In theatre the character speaking on the stage is the one an audience cannot help but look at. In film the director decides who the audience is to look at. Often it will be the character who is not speaking who the camera needs to see for the **reaction shot** to what is being said. **Thus, stars will often ask for their dialogue to be reduced in the script, so they can be listening and reacting, gaining more screen time on themselves.** The complete opposite to the theatre actor who wants all the lines, because there is only one place the audience is likely to be looking, that is at the speaking actor. (Unless of course someone is upstaging them with visual business of their own, as I once witnessed with an actor playing with a handkerchief!). Upstaging is not possible on film – the director decides who to look at. Stealing a scene with a screen performance is its blameless equivalent and of course that's what stars are made of.

Reaction Shots

Q. Why the reaction shot?

A. If the camera is on a character in a single shot making a speech, once they have started to speak, we know what that character looks and sounds like. We then want to know what those listening are thinking. The director will cut to their reactions to signify this. We the audience know from the sound of the speaking character's delivery what they are thinking and feeling. We the viewers need to know what the listening audience in the scene is thinking and feeling. Encourage your 'reacting' actors to react.

Director and Actor note:

Just 'thinking it' may not be enough. Time to direct or self-direct for a bit of 'over re-acting'! Reaction shots are vital for- well reactions. Speak soft – Think loud. Show don't just think it.

Helping Actors Be Natural

Actor note: make sure you also read the following.

Q. How can I direct actors to appear to be natural in the environment of a scene?

A. Props, props, props. If an actor has not found themselves something that their character would have with them, then give it to them (within reason). In your every day & night travels in the world, watch everyone around you, and yourself, we are all of us usually fidgeting with something while engaged in conversation or thought.

The great director/writer Billy Wilder in the classic film 'Some Like It Hot' gave Jack Lemmon for the 'I'm engaged/I'm a boy' scene a pair of maracas and said "In between each line play them". Lemmon said that at the time "I thought he's nuts – he's really blown his lid" but in retrospect "The scene was great. Billy Wilder was great again".[3]

Here it is – Comedy at its best

https://youtu.be/rSOsXYemTuw

Of course this could be a nightmare for continuity, but we now know how to lessen that likely error.

Meryl Streep once said that Robert De Niro was so obsessive about detail that for their movie *Falling In Love* (1984) he examined 40 different but near-identical jackets before deciding which one perfectly suited his character. De Niro confirmed this saying "Somehow that particular piece of clothing, that particular something, that particular prop opens up a subconscious door or avenue to things that you've accumulated over your life that made impressions on you, that you associate with using that particular thing, that you bring back. It comes back to you. And you might not even know why. So it helps give you what you feel is right for that character."[4]

---

[3] CARDULLO, B. et al (1998) Playing To The Camera. Yale University Press. p.270

[4] http://www.dailymail.co.uk/home/moslive/article-2131682/Piers-Morgan-interviewing-Robert-De-Niro-How-I-answer-sighed-actor-Please-I-silently-begged.html#ixzz3cLnwKvyf

> **Director and Actor note:** 'if you have the time on the set - I like to tell the actors to try anything - have the time to fail - go ahead try, this try that - you need that freedom - you have to give them that freedom' Martin Scorsese Master Class.
>
> **N.B.** make sure you make it a take - otherwise you may have missed the gold that has both director and actor looking inspired.

Cheating

Q. **How do I, as a director, get what I want into a shot?**

A. Cheating:

There is little real when it comes to the seeming reality of film (and that goes for the realest, of what is supposed to be real – documentary filmmaking – but that is another story).

When shooting, there is only one place a director should be looking. The temptation is to look beyond the camera, to the actors performing in front of it.

Your only concern once the camera is rolling is to look at **The Monitor** which tells you exactly what is in **THE FRAME.**

a/ Always with more than one person in a shot i.e., a 2 Shot, 3 shot or more, try to 'cheat' your subjects into the shot with as tight (close) a shot as looks comfortable in the frame. This may not be comfortable for your actors, who may feel that they are invading each other's space. A distance of 3 feet and no less is considered as close as we feel comfortable with unless emotionally involved. For the camera that may not look close enough.

If it looks right in the frame, convince your actors likewise. The fatal error you as a director might make is to widen the shot to make the actors feel comfortable.

b/ In a MCU it may be that the prop they have felt comfortable with in the Master Shot is not visible in the frame in the MCU being just below the bottom of it. Ask your actors to cheat it up so that you can see it. Maybe the holding of a glass they are drinking from etc. Again, this may feel uncomfortable for your actor but if it looks better in the frame, convince them of that.

Director note: sometimes it is necessary to direct as in the silent movie days. i.e. telling the actor while the camera is rolling exactly what to do.

'Put the cigarette closer to your face - take a drag - gently blow smoke out - flick in ash tray...'etc.

Now, it is best, to explain to the actor that you are going to give verbal directions like that, otherwise as with Liam Neeson in *Schindler's List* (1993) above, although it was Steven Spielberg giving direction who did just that, said he was irritated and felt his expertise as an actor was in question.

It was only on seeing the end result that he appreciated exactly how necessary Spielberg's intervention had been with, smoke - cigarette - and himself perfectly placed in each frame throughout the restaurant scene introducing his character Schindler to the audience.

https://youtu.be/32j4zj0U-2w

c/ Cheating a physical character trait into shot is also important. If a character has been wringing their hands with nerves in the Master Shot, ask the actor to cheat this trait into the frame of the MCU as is shown here where James Stewart is having a nervous breakdown in *It's A Wonderful Life* (1946) (DVD. 00 .31.54).

It would be no use to an audience signifying his nervousness, if his hand was out of shot.

Director and Actor note:

Director

Always let the talent know the size of shot so that they may adapt their performance to it vocally and physically with props etc.

Actor

Always ask what size of shot you are being shot in so that you may adapt your performance to it vocally and physically with props etc.

Director & Actor

In the frame of the shot from Mid Shot to Extreme Close Up: know that eyes can be effective glancing up above the frame, as well as the usual down and sideways.

Director & Actor

Make sure movement is into the shot and out of the shot. Not stilted waiting for the word action and cut. Again, the editor will love you for this and directors love to be...well, love to be right! If you are going to be one and the same - director and editor - then you'll certainly love yourself even more - and Actor – your performance will be real with movement.

N.B. Always try and pre-empt questions your audience may ask for an answer to. With pause and rewind that has never been more necessary. Filmmakers of old could have had no idea that modern technology would allow the general public to examine every frame. You do!

Acting Talent

Q. **What makes a good actor?**

A.

a/ Imagination.

b/ Good actors appear to think quickly; vocally they can change gear effortlessly i.e., fast, slow – loud, soft – happy, sad etc... while keeping the pace and mood.

Q. **What makes a star?**

A. Personality: that indescribable something that the camera loves, that is unique to their personas and cannot be imagined as anyone but who they are - Cary Grant, James Stewart, Ingrid Bergman, Greta Garbo, Katherine Hepburn, Humphrey Bogart, Marilyn Monroe, Jackie Chan, Eddie Murphy, Al Pacino,

Michael Caine, Morgan Freeman, Halle Berry, Whitney Houston, Dwayne Johnson (The Rock), Will Smith etc., .they play to their type with little variation and audiences love them for it.

Q. What if an actor's performance is not appearing to be real?

A. Bad actors signal that they are acting. It's what I call 'Acting Acting', inflicting emotion on the text. To stop this, direct by saying "just say the words/lines without emoting – let the words act you'. This will usually work if a performance is not seeming to be real.

Director note: try not to make it obvious to your actor that you are not feeling their performance. Make an excuse along the lines of a technical difficulty for the reason you had to cut, needing another take. Whilst that is pretending to be solved have a quiet chat with them offering your suggestion that they might like to try…

N.B. an actor has to expose their inner soul to the world. It is a sensitive craft that a director needs to navigate with care to avoid causing emotional paralysis to their performance.

Veteran Director John Boorman's trick was…

'Actors need to be able to trust their director. If you want to get the best out of them adjust something in their orbit like their hair just before a take.

By doing something like that, the actor feels you are watching everything.

For an actor to jump off a cliff emotionally they have to trust you. Getting the trust of an actor is the most important thing for a director to do.

There are two kinds of acting. The survival acting where the actor says I know how to get through this scene without making a fool of myself. Then there is the acting where the actor is going to take chances emotionally. He or she will only do that if they have trust in the director. Watching out for stray hairs is one way of helping to get that trust'.

John Boorman (2020) *The Film Programme* BBC Radio 4 iPlayer Podcast (accessed 11/03/20)

Cinematography Q & A

Cinematography the art of Lighting

Q. Do I need to use lighting?

A. Yes, yes, yes! It may surprise you to know, that even 'reality shows' i.e. Made in Chelsea, Come Dine With Me, Love Island, The Only Way Is Essex etc., pre-light scenes. Why? Because natural light is not enough for the camera. You may think it is. You will look and may conclude that there is plenty of light. Now squint your eyes

see where the light and shade is? The shade will be too much. The responsibility for this when filming is that of the Director Of Photography (DOP) also known as Cinematographer. The person in charge of setting the lights up is the Gaffer. Your film will have no atmosphere if you fail to pay attention to 'painting with light'. Make sure you understand its power and thank Nikola Tesla pictured below not Thomas Edison!

Director note:

a/ Most professional solid-state cameras have a 'Zebra' setting that will show where over exposure is taking place. For safety use it. You cannot fix over exposure in the edit!

b/ If filming outside, use the **camera's viewfinder** with an external portable monitor attached. If you use the LCD on the camera **cover it from light** or you will find the lighting around the picture either shows it is bright enough or not, whichever way, when you get the files uploaded in the edit, you may be disappointed with it either being too dark or over-exposed.

c/ Failing to light the eyes of your talent unless intentionally to hide their face – is a sin. The eyes are your film talent's most important tool of their trade. You deny your audience an understanding of the characters being portrayed. Dialogue is often secondary to reaction that glance; that stare; that teardrop etc. We need to see it – not to have to imagine it. Lights, lights, lights!

Cinematography

Q. What does good cinematography look like?

A. Behind every great director there is a cinematographer/director of photography (DOP) responsible for tone, atmosphere and emotion that they create with control over composition, contrast, and colour. When you see it in combination with all other movie-ing parts it is 'breath-taking'.

It started with the director D W Griffiths and his DOP Billy Bitzer who began collaborating on a silent movie *Pippa Passes* in 1909. Bitzer "developed camera techniques that set the standard for all future motion pictures."[5] Filming using artificial light rather than daylight.

Bitzer lit closeups

Intolerance (1916) and...long shots to create mood

---

[5] Encyclopædia Britannica, Micropædia, Vol. II, p51

He created soft focus with diffuser screens to combat the hard light of carbon arc spotlights and reflected light with bounce boards.

Carbon arc studio spotlight

Q. How did they film before artificial light?

A. In the early days of studio filming sets were built on revolving stages in the open (sometimes with a glass roof) so that the stage could be turned throughout the day towards the sunlight (which was plentiful) in California - leading to the region of Hollywood becoming the movie Mecca.

It was also the reason why although commercial lighting had been available worldwide since 1879 - that filmmakers (requiring an enormous amount of light because of film's slow speed at the time) avoided the cumbersome and expensive carbon arc spotlight until 30 years later in favour of a free sun.

Artificial light - camera lenses and cameras became more advanced with each decade, enabling the craft of the following masters of cinematography to create truly 'breath-taking' cinematography that complements their director's vision. If you have not already seen their work it is worth searching out to observe many quality films they have made, often for the same director...

DOP: John Alton - Dir: Vincente Minnelli - *An American in Paris* (1951). Book *Painting with Light* Quote: 'It's not what you light it's what you DON'T light.' See *The Big Combo* (1955) with his spectacular film-noir lighting.

DOP: Roger Deakins - Dir: Frank Darabont - *The Shawshank Redemption* (1994). Dir: Sam Mendes *1917* (2019) Oscar for Best Cinematography. Simplistic lighting design, often using only one or two lights.

DOP: Gregg Toland - Dir: Orson Welles - *Citizen Kane* (1941) Deep-focus cinematography, depicting a broad and clear foreground, middle ground, and background.

DOP: Robert Burks - Dir: Alfred Hitchcock - *Rear Window* (1954, Technicolor). Played an integral part in creating the brooding, tension-laden atmosphere of the director's best work between 1954 and 1964.

DOP: Freddie Young - Dir: David Lean - *Lawrence of Arabia* (1962, CinemaScope). Book: The Work of the Motion Picture Cameraman.[6]

DOP: Vittorio Storaro - Dir: Francis Ford Coppola - *Apocalypse Now* (1979). Scenes are often illuminated with light from the side instead of overhead. For interiors the main source of light appeared to come through windows; for exteriors, the sun low in the sky.

DOP: Sven Nykvist - Dir: Ingmar Bergman - *Cries and Whispers* (1972). "Today we make everything so complicated. The lighting, the cameras, the acting. It has taken me thirty years to arrive at simplicity." He revolutionised the way faces are shot in close-up with Bergman's psychological drama *Persona* (1966).[7]

---

[6] Young F. Petzold P. (1972) *The Work of the Motion Picture Cameraman* - Focal Press, London.

[7] Borden, D.M., 1977. Bergman's style and the facial icon. Quarterly Review of Film Studies 2, 42–55. https://doi.org/10.1080/10509207709391332

Persona (1966)

Persona (1966)

DOP: Kazuo Miyagawa - Dir: Akira Kurosawa – *Rashomon* (1950) noted for his tracking shots and mastery of black and white cinematography.

DOP: - Janusz Kaminski - Dir: Steven Spielberg - *Schindler's List* (1993). "Cinematography is the art of light and shadows, visual metaphors and nuance." Imdb [2018]

DOP: - Maryse Alberti - Dir: Darren Aronofsky - *The Wrestler* (2008). She was the first contemporary female cinematographer featured on the cover of *American Cinematographer*

DOP: Arthur Edeson - Dir: Michael Curtiz - *Casablanca* (1943).

Casablanca (1943) Ingrid Bergman

Actor note: make friends with your cinematographer. Ingrid Bergman was shot mainly from her preferred left side, often with a softening gauze filter and with catchlights or 'obie' to place a reflection in the eyes to make her eyes sparkle; the whole effect was designed to make her face seem "ineffably sad and tender and nostalgic"[8]

Casablanca (1943) Humphrey Bogart

---

[8] Ebert, Roger. Commentary to *Casablanca* (Two-Disc Special Edition DVD).

> **Director note:** new directors are often shy of taking close up shots - yet they show the inner psychology of a character's 'emotion' when we are able to invade their space - don't deny your viewers getting up close for pillow talk.

Type of Lights

Q. **What type of lights do you recommend?**

A. Light Emitting Diode (LED): LED lights can be daylight - or tungsten - balanced, sometimes switchable or having a variable colour temperature. Some have variable colour through the entire Red Green Blue (RGB) spectrum, which is something not possible with any other lighting technology.

Some offer effects: Storm - Cop Car - Candle Light - Hard Disco - Soft Disco - Monitor and Multi Flash with extra lighting effects for matching Sodium Vapour Light - Metal Halide Light - Fluorescent Light and Street Light.

They create a small amount of heat - have a long crystal bulb life - use little electricity - have exceptional battery life - create a soft light with no need for diffusing with a light box.

LED lights all have intensity controls on them saving money on the need to purchase dimmer controls.

An LED Fresnel has a narrow to wide beam with manual brightness dial

Being able to run LEDs with <u>battery power</u> for outside locations is another major advantage. Never let it be said that you don't need lights for outside daylight shoots for complete control over your cinematography.

Plus LED's have a long lifespan - are environmentally friendly - are insensitive to shock - safer with no risk of explosion - and safe to move instantly to new locations there being no need to wait 10 minutes for them to cool down.

Q. Are LED lighting kits expensive?

A. No more than standard Ianiro or Arri tungsten studio lamp kits - but yes - to do the job effectively they can be - perhaps all of the above for the price of a high-mileage second hand car. A couple of alternatives could be to hire, or if safety-checked, buy second-hand.

Q. Could domestic lights be used to keep costs down?

A. Yes - the following type of 'practical lighting' was used by Robert Rodriguez ...

> **Director note:** filmmaker Robert Rogriguez records guerrilla methods in his book *Rebel Without A Crew*,[9] a lesson in self-sacrifice to create his first feature film that saw him successfully achieve a welcome into the Hollywood pantheon.

Builder's Work Light: from DIY store that can have either tungsten (indoor colour temperature) or daylight (outdoor colour temperature) balanced bulbs. Good for day and night shoots on a budget - price of two large pizzas from a well-known takeaway.

Rechargeable LED Work Light: (6000K Daylight color temperature)

Domestic LED Bulbs: various power and kelvin colour balance available for the price of a café toasted panini for 2. To be placed in domestic fittings.

---

[9] Rodriguez R. (2018) *Rebel Without A Crew*. Rob Smart Publication

LED Clamp Spotlight: versatile and clampable into various positions using stands etc...all for the price of a good book *Cinematography for Directors*.

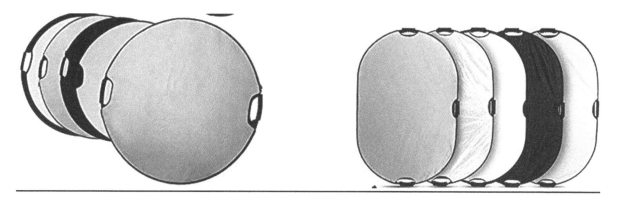

Diffusers & Reflectors: diffusers to spread cover to alarger areas with soft light and reflectors to reflect natural or artificial light onto the subject.

These systems come in packs of 5 - Black/Gold/Silver/White/Translucent

Circular 110 cm - Oblong 80 × 120 cm. for the price of a single Indian takeaway.

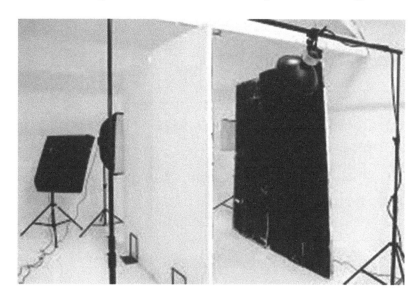

Bounce boards: polystyrene boards from a DIY store 6 × 4 can be useful to reflect larger areas for the price of a bottle of prosecco.

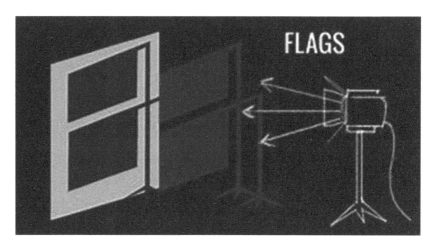

Flags: to block light or deepen shadows

Goboes: for creating patterns and shadows

> **Director note:** directors Stanley Kubrick & David Fincher have been known to use natural 'practical lights'.
>
> The hours of sunrise (dawn) and sunset (dusk) are known as the magic hours for light - **golden hour** after dawn or before sunset, or the **blue hour** at dawn or dusk. *The Revenant* (2015) was shot entirely in natural light.

White Balance

Q. **What is White Balance?**

A. Our brains adjust colour as we encounter different environments. The camera cannot think and needs to be able to gauge correct colour by being told what white is for each different environment. This can be done manually by holding up a white or light grey card in front of your actors, zooming in and filling the screen with at least two thirds of the card and pressing the camera's manual balance button. If filming indoors with daylight coming through windows put blue daylight gels on your lights and <u>only then do the manual white balance, with the gels on.</u>

Q. **Should I always manually set the white balance?**

A. That is a question all self-respecting cinematographers would not need to ask, however sometimes (though seldom) location situations may need to be rushed and the following may be accessed.

Cameras also have an auto pre-set switch that allows the camera a choice of 3200 degrees Kelvin for indoors and 5600 degrees Kelvin for outdoors. If your picture looks very blue when outside, you will know it is on the indoor setting and needs changing. If reddish when filming indoors then you have got it on an outdoor setting. Always think of the big number 5600K representing outside open spaces and the smaller number 3200K for the indoor setting.

N.B. Some indoor fluorescent light tubes are special daylight tubes that you may find installed in certain indoor locations to avoid a condition affecting staff known as Seasonal Affective Disorder (SAD). In that case the pre-set outdoor white balance 5600K would be selected.

Q. **What if I want to film at night?**

A. One way is to film **Day for Night**. You set the cameras pre-set to 3200K the indoor setting. Outside that will give you a blue hue. Turn the iris down to as dark as it will allow. <u>Make sure you do not film the sky in the shots and that you turn on lights that would all be on at night, cars lights etc.</u>

Director note: If you do shoot at night or early dawn or early evening, make sure you have an additional light on your actors' faces that is not too blue so that the viewer can read their faces, especially the eyes. In the edit colour grading can then be added if needed to create more of the atmosphere of night.

Camera Q & A

Q. What camera?

A. For a cinematic look (film look) a Digital Single Lens Reflex (DSLR), Black Magic, Sony, Canon, Panasonic or for the price of a top of the range Tesla Car you might like to film with one of the following Hollywood preferred cameras compared here

Red Vs Arri

https://youtu.be/Znu-c4R9Pws

The bottom line is, you need a digital make of camera body that can accept a variety of lens types that may be changed to accommodate the director & director of photography's vision (elaborated on in the previous cinematography section).

Above the Canon EOS C100: note the handle with 2 XLR inputs for professional balanced synchronised sound-recording.

Lenses

Q. **What lenses?**

A. Prime Lenses

Q. **What is a 'Prime lens'?**

A. Prime Lenses for image quality in narrative filmmaking.

Q. **What is a 'Prime' lens?**

A. It's not a Zoom lens! It has a fixed focal length allowing for much more sharpness than the aforementioned and will allow for a faster shutter speed in low light manufactured with a wider aperture allowing for more light. The faster shutter speed is important because when you use a wide aperture it may be too bright. Increasing the speed will allow you to reduce the light. Conversely the more light needed will allow you to reduce the shutter speed to a minimum 1/50th for moving talent.

The following 3 lens sizes will provide the necessary tools for creative vision.

a/ Prime 24 mm Wide Angle

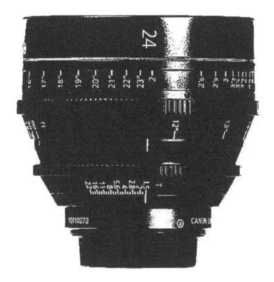

Provides a broader perspective to capture grand vistas or small interiors. Also known as short lens due to its short focal length.

Ideal for:
Deep focus
Wide shots
Master & Long Shots

Long depth of field (DoF) all subjects sharp

N.B. Never use near an actor unless you want them to look fat and distorted!

b/ Prime 50mm Normal Lens

Fixed focal length lens.

Normal lens: mimicking almost what the human eye sees.

c/ Prime 85mm Short Telephoto

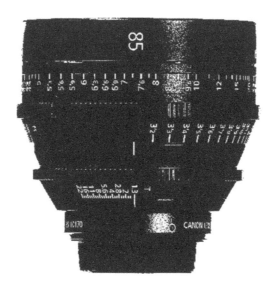

Fixed focus. A natural angle of view and perspective.

Ideal for:
Low light shooting.
Shallow depth of field.
Shallow focus for 'bokeh'

Bokeh

Q. What is bokeh (pronounced 'Boh' -then- 'Ke' as in Ke-pt)?

A. This is 'bokeh' written in its original language ボケ: that may, if you don't read the language, look like a 'blur' which is exactly what it means in Japanese! It is when the background (Fig 1), or background and foreground (Fig 2) are not in focus drawing attention to the subject/s who will be in perfect focus.

Fig. 1 *The King's Speech* (2010)

Fig. 2 *The King's Speech* (2010)

It is the classic cinematographic look that until digital technology allowed would have required film cameras and film stock at unattainable prices for an independent novice filmmaker.

Q. How do I create the bokeh look?

A. It's all in the Depth of Feld (DoF) that you control with the selected lens and aperture setting. Fig.4 shows the varying degrees of f/stops. The lower figure being the widest aperture.

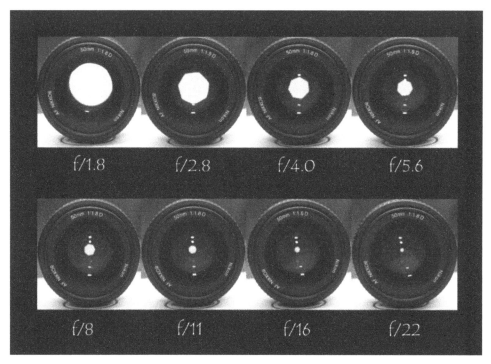

Fig. 4

With an 85 mm Short Telephoto Lens you might expect in Fig.5 the following to be in focus within the DoF with the bokeh (ボケ) area in foreground and background. The vertical line shows a longer distance will be in focus in the background.

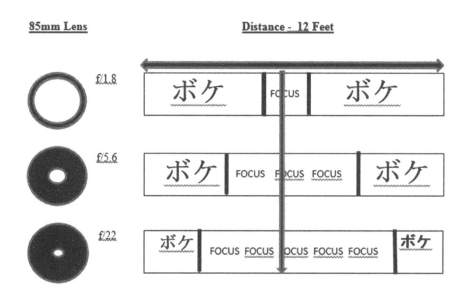

Fig. 5

Pulling Focus

Q. **What does pulling focus mean?**

A. You may have one character in shot. Another character joins the frame in the background. To accentuate their presence focus is 'Pulled' so that the foreground character becomes out of focus in favour of the background character being in focus.

This also can happen in reverse.

> **Director note:** Don't pull focus too often in a scene. Only use it to make a point. I watched an episode of the BBC's Downton Abbey where two characters in conversation throughout a 2-minute scene repeatedly had the focus pulled on their individual performances. It was irritating, boring and unnecessary. If we as an audience become aware of camera tricks, it is a distraction from your story telling. Don't fall into the trap.

Sound

Q. **Why were silent movies silent?**

A. As soon as moving images, at the beginning part of the Nineteenth century were able to be edited to tell a story, the missing ingredient of synchronised dialogue sound was experimented with in short films but without much success.

It would be 40 yrs. from the oldest surviving footage of film *Roundhay Garden* (1888)

https://youtu.be/J0bHbKrhmTQ

created by French inventor Louis Le Prince, before in 1927 a full-length feature was released that had a recorded musical score and synched sound effects but still no spoken dialogue relying on the integral silent movie **intertitles** Fig. 1 to inform the story, it can be seen in the following QR, the romantic silent movie melodrama *Sunrise* (1927)

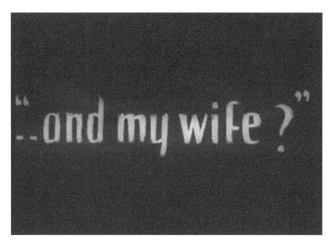

Fig. 1

https://youtu.be/z-8_bLPvca4

Q. **When was dialogue first recorded on film?**

A. The Jazz Singer (1927)

https://youtu.be/cBwuNHJCHxl

is acknowledged as the first feature film to have synchronised dialogue, albeit fleetingly, as most of the film is silent with intertitles.

This was followed by *Lights of New York* (1928)

https://youtu.be/4PNBSLjmQh0

a first full length talking feature film, that on occasion had to have intertitles to progress the story, when technically recording of dialogue was restricted by the recording system.

Q. **What was the first recording system used?**

A. The recording system was a **Vitaphone** seen here endorsed by Warner Bros Studios during 1926–1931.

The sound was recorded separately from the film stock to a phonograph record that can be seen on the turntable in the centre of this picture.

The noise from a Camera and Vitaphone system combined, meant that the Vitaphone had to be in a soundproofed booth, while a microphone in the studio, had to be hidden on set at a distance from the Camera but near enough for the talent to be heard.

> **Director & Actor note:** Watch this scene from *Singin' in the Rain* (1952) also directed by *Charade's* director Stanley Donen that comically addresses the trials and tribulations of recording the early talkies.
>
>
>
> https://youtu.be/KOfwio9lJe8

Away from Hollywood, Alfred Hitchcock's *Blackmail* (1929) feature

📱 Blackmail

https://youtu.be/Bt1XgUvjWd0

was the first British/European film to adopt sound.

Recording sound to film stock with optical sound tracks had become possible in the 1920's allowing for instant synchronisation.

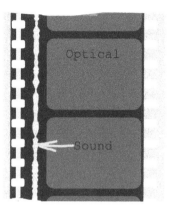

However, the quality of sound was secondary to the sound on disc system plus a lot more expensive. Studios stuck with Vitaphone type sound to disc systems until the mid 1930's.

It was expensive, not just for the creators but for the end user, Theatres/Cinemas, who had to invest in technology for their audiences to hear. Duly, studios printed dual versions to accommodate their clients, giving them the choice of silent or talky.

Director & Actor note: The introduction of recording synchronised dialogue sound set the cinematographer, actor and director's art into a retrograde 'motionless' state.

Having developed film language with editors and directors discovering the freedom of moving the camera in silent films away from the initial static proscenium-theatre camera position, to the variety of shots that we recognise today of close ups, reverse shots and spectacular stunts, such as this Harold Lloyd stunt effect in *Safety Last* (1923)

📱 Safety Last

https://youtu.be/pM7WEB2W2gU

The camera again was restricted, not this time by naivety, but by having to watch conversations taking place in the vicinity of the immovable cumbersome sound recording apparatus that had to be hidden on set.

There is no better example of this restriction, than watching the great film actress Greta Garbo in the following scene from *Anna Christie* (1930)

https://youtu.be/GLiEPy8SZ4s

N.B. as time went by multiple cameras were used to make up for the loss of mobility until sound equipment was minimised.

The way was led by Director Rouben Mamoulian with

Applause (1929) who shows spectacular movement here filming from a nunnery to a city with dialogue and sound effects

https://youtu.be/YUZ8IHGZcvM

Q. **Is it true that silent film stars became unemployable in the talkies because their voices didn't fit how they were imagined to sound?**

A. It is possible that some had 'funny voices', or more charitably, a voice that did not fit what their audiences had imagined, along the lines of the *Singin in the Rain* parody.

John Gilbert known as 'The Great Lover' during his silent movie stardom (rivalling at the time even Rudolph Valentino who had acquired the same appellation with his movies), had aspersions cast that "John Gilbert had a squeaky voice", by those that had not heard him in an early talky, such as the following *Downstairs* (1932)

https://youtu.be/B8-wFceDRpw

where it is obviously not true.

Greta Garbo (1905 -1990) who was a Swedish American, started her career in silent films to become ranked 5th on The American Film Institute list, of the greatest female stars of Classic Hollywood Cinema.

Garbo was lucky with her accent adding to her charisma, others who spoke no American English although being known for playing American characters, became no longer castable as such.

> **Director & Actor note:** many greats of the silent era did have their status wane, no less so than many of the great comic performers of the time, Buster Keaton, Harold Lloyd et al.
>
> This though, was not because of the introduction of sound, more the entertainment industries ineluctable need to find the next 'flavour of the month'.
>
> One of the great filmmakers and stars from this era who refused to adopt sound in its early stages was Charlie Chaplin. *City Lights* (1931) and *Modern Times* (1936) were both without dialogue. Eventually he relented continuing to be able to create a lasting body of work, writing, directing and composing up to his last film *A Countess from Hong Kong* in 1967.

Q. Today, how important is sound in relation to cinematography?

A. You can get away with some bad cinematography in a few shots with good sound. You cannot get away with good cinematography at anytime with bad sound.

So much attention by manufacturers has been paid to the picture quality cameras produce that sound has been left with less attention. The low end DSLR camera is a case in point: fantastic control over the depth of field leading to cinematic shots.

However, to achieve quality sound you need to add quality sound equipment that will need to be synchronised to the image in the editing timeline having recorded separately with a sound mixer and carried out the professional method of using a Slate/Clapperboard for every shot (see appendix 3 for correct use).

For good quality sound in budget/guerrilla/indie filmmaking (if no sound mixing equipment is at hand) only use professional cinematic cameras that have integral XLR Inputs as seen below

Never buy or hire a camera that has a mini sound jack input. Only use a camera's internal mic system to synchronise a separate sound mixer's recording in the edit that certain software can synchronise the mixer recording to.

Q. **What skill does the person in charge of sound need?**

A. With dialogue the microphone's distance to the talent will depend on the size of the shot. With a Medium Close Up and Close Up it is vital to get the microphone on a boom pole as close to, in front of those speaking, as the top of the frame will allow

Q. How loud should actors talk if the microphone is that close?

A. Sound advice for Talent, Directors and Sound Operators: only allow dialogue to be projected to the distance of the microphone. Do not let a theatre performance projecting to the rest of the crew be filmed. With less projection, the face becomes more expressive, giving more emotional information to the camera and thus viewer.

Director and Actor note:

a/ be aware that with the closeness of the microphone, the talent should be speaking more quietly – but they will possibly also be speaking more slowly. You may need to ask them to increase the pace and intensity – not the volume!

b/ make sure your actors are speaking clearly. Not mumbling. Reality incoherence is not welcome to audiences that may need to pause and rewind several times (if they can be bothered that is).

c/ directors: remember the more you have read the script and the more you hear it spoken, any incoherence may be going unnoticed by yourself because you know it so well.

Q. What microphone?

A. Use a quality 'short shotgun' microphone with an XLR cable from the camera to a boom pole. Quality costs money but will save a lot of heartache. Cheap microphones are poorly engineered, screws fall out and produce the one issue you are trying to avoid – bad rattling sound.

Q. What boom should I use?

A. Be careful – once again money buys quality – cheap ones rattle and fall apart. Carbon Fibre ones are lighter and more reliable.

Hire or Buy?

Q. Should I hire or buy equipment?

A. Hiring is a very good option, especially as technology changes by the second.

Advantages:

a/ access to the latest equipment with advice and choice.

b/ back-up should technical faults arise.

c/ handing equipment back means you have not invested in a depreciating commodity.

Disadvantages:

a/ you'll need some time to familiarise crew with new equipment.

b/ will have to stick to the time frame of the hire (within budget).

c/ you may fall in love with it and not want to return it!

d/ ...which is why in most instances, you will need to prove your identity, with accompanying security of a hefty deposit and provide insurance cover during the hire period.

Post-Production Q & A

Editing Q & A

Director and actor note:

'...you can ruin a movie with editing - you can make it better - you can ruin an actor's performance... so it's very important that we take this raw lump of material that 200 people have created and then we shape it like a sculptor into something that works as a film', Thelma Schoonmaker *Wolf of Wall Street* (2013) Editor on editing.

Thelma S

https://youtu.be/Xilu7KSxcm4

Editing Software

Adobe Premiere

Q. What software should I use?

A. Today, Adobe Premiere Pro with the Adobe Suite offers the most creative professional option for a reasonable budget. Integration between many complementary programmes that include Adobe After Effects and Adobe Photoshop have made it a choice for many departments at the BBC. You purchase it from the Adobe Cloud paying a monthly or yearly subscription. The disadvantage with this is that software updates are frequent and may lead your computer to not having the power to accommodate the frequent creative innovations. *Deadpool* (2016) was edited on Premiere Pro.

Final Cut Pro has been popular amongst universities and is another option, but unlike Adobe it will require plug- ins to compete with Adobe. It is also only available for Apple Mac Computers whereas Adobe cater for both PC and Mac.

Avid Media Composer was the first non- linear editing system. It is what the above are based on, and still today it is the crème de la crème. If you can afford it.

Whichever you choose, make sure the computer/laptop is a high enough specification to cope with the demands of editing moving image. To guarantee the specification being suitable find one of the several specialist companies selling moving image editing hardware. 32 gigs of Ram are a must.

Technique

Q. What technique would you recommend to edit?

A.

a/ you may have every shot planned and filmed according to the method I outline in Scene 1. In which case set the shots out on the timeline as designed.

However, you may also like to try the following method in the edit:

b/ with the script in front of you, lay on the timeline a rough edit of the master shots for each scene. That will tell you the continuum of the story. When that is done the fun starts.

Editing needs to be intuitive:

Now watch the master shot timeline stopping when you feel it would be interesting to see a Medium Close Up, Close Up, or Reaction Shot etc., of a character. Insert it and carry on. When you play it back, again intuition will tell you how long each shot needs to be, before a cut to another view. Eventually it will appear seamless (as long as continuity has been seamless).

> **Director note:** If you give the same footage to different editors without a storyboard their intuition will create a choice of different shots showing a surprising variety of inspired interpretations. The art is subjective.
>
> '...sometimes when Scorsese comes in I've created 4 different edits of a scene for him because there are so many options... ' Thelma Schoonmaker *Wolf of Wall Street* (2013) Editor on editing. **https://youtu.be/Xilu7KSxcm4**
>
> **N.B.** she is a witness for the prosecution against diehard storyboard or shooting script adherents: those premiere decisions, need not remain as the only option in the edit.

Zippy Zappy Zediting

Q. what is 'Zippy Zappy Zediting'?

A. it is my term for - ways of moving content in a shot or scene that has a style of its own.

Many styles can be achieved simplistically without first resorting to motion graphics where indeed more spectacular effects can be introduced that are worth researching beyond the confines of this book (tutorials on YouTube are plentiful).

For now - try experimenting creating footage that you speed up (fast Motion) - slow down (slow Motion) - reverse - time lapse - hyper lapse - jump cut - in a shot or scene.

Examples:

- **Entrance and exit shots for comic effect:** the camera is set up for a Master Shot in a sitting room- we see 3 characters enter a room and sit on the sofa.

    Style in the edit: **fast forward their entrance** to sitting on the sofa - play the scene at normal pace - **fast forward their exit.**

- **Jump cut:** camera watches a character on the move.

    Style in the edit: create the scene into **Jump Cuts** by taking out 25 or 50 frames then leaving 25 or 50 and so on intermittently with optionally speeding the footage up.

    An alternative way is on a single shot in the edit to cut **zoom in** then cut and onwards - or cut **zoom out** then cut and onwards. This is very effective with the character's dialogue continuing to flow. To clarify as follows...

Master Shot with them talking - CUT ZOOM IN

Key to this size. Play and CUT

ZOOM key to this size. Play and CUT   ZOOM and key to this size.

Example

Jump Cut

https://youtu.be/HnWL_bGCY_g

Repeat shock shot: 3 Cameras film action of something that happens so fast it might be missed. Integral to the story it is repeated from different angles and at different speeds e.g. The end scene of *The Usual Suspects* (1995) sees the character drop the mug he is drinking from as he has a realisation.

Style in the edit: each angle is repeated with us seeing it smash 3 times on the floor splattering the contents from different angles - the first shot of the drop to smash is in slow motion.

Example

https://youtu.be/Z8YuAHiWoRw

The same technique could be used on an actor reacting to seeing something shocking, for instance.

- **Freeze frame:** just what it says used to great effect in *Goodfellas* and many other Martin Scorsese directed films edited by his renowned sole editor Thelma Schoonmaker.

Transitions

Q. **What are transitions?**

A. A <u>change</u> from one <u>form</u> or <u>type</u> to another, or the <u>process</u> by which this <u>happens</u>: (Cambridge Dictionary). In film, from one scene or sequence to another...

Too often novices to editing fall in love with the hundreds of various transitional designs available in editing software. They are to be avoided unless progressing the action without the distraction of 'look how clever my editing is with this fancy transitional Segway into the next scene'.

> **Director note:** transitions should not be welcomed between every cut or indeed every scene. A clean cut will usually be enough to transport the viewer to another scene by dint of the fact that the scenery is different.

Examples to try:

- **Time passing/montage:** one way within a scene could be - have the camera locked off in a Master Shot - see character/s in one position - cross fade - to them being in another position and so on: accompanied by the **sound** of a ticking clock.

  A **cross fade** or an **in and out fade** is generally only to be used to show the passing of time as in the end montage scene of *American Beauty* (1999).

- **Match cut:** you can see a masterful one in Charade where in the mortuary the body in the freezer drawer is being slid back into the freezer, cutting to the Inspector's Office draw being slid open.

  It can be can be viewed using the QR code here

https://archive.org/details/Charade19631280x696

Mortuary to Inspectors Office at 9.13 - 9.57

- **J cut:** the end of the *Charade* Embassy scene has a perfect example of this (take a look at it using the QR above at 25.09 - 25.14) The sound of the Punch and Judy fairground music plays in while still on Regina's Close Up in the Embassy office, then the scene cuts to the fair.

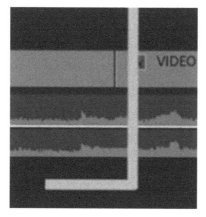

The sound from the next visual scene comes in before the cut to it.

- **L cut:** in Charade the hotel chambermaid's scream at seeing the drowned character in the bath carries over into the next scene of his body having been placed on a bed. (QR above at 106 - 108)

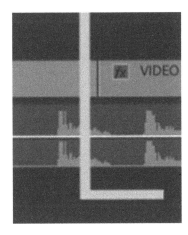

The sound from current shot carries over into the next scene after the cut to it.

Director note:

Both 'J' cuts and 'L' cuts are a necessity in dialogue scenes for the all-important **reaction** shots mentioned earlier.

The 'instincts' of director and editor need at this point to be at their creative best. While watching and listening to the footage from the assembled shots 'instinct' will let you know when you want to be seeing the **reaction** of the other character making use of 'J' or 'L' cuts. These are **moments** that will not necessarily be in your storyboard or shooting script.

Parallel Editing/Cross cutting

Q. What is Parallel/Cross cutting Editing?

A. A tremendous way to build tension. Alternate between two locations and characters who are eventually going to meet up unexpectedly (too soon). The man on the way back from the pub – the wife preparing a poisonous concoction for him to drink on his return. See script 'Give Peace A Chance' (**p. 247**)

Editing your own work

Q. If I am the director and editor or even the writer or actor what will I have to be aware of?

A. You will need an objective opinion on the final cut. It will probably be over long and unclear in places where you know the script inside out. Listen to the objective opinion. Ignore it at your peril. A director's cut is always longer, not necessarily for the better.

Q. What if I also act in the film?

A. If you are also an actor, then my advice is let someone else edit your scenes. As an actor you will be self-critical cutting out much of the wheat in favour of the chaff because you don't like the way you said a line or the way you looked.

Director note: editor Walter Murch [on the evolution of the average shot length] The average shot length of *The Birth of a Nation* (1915) is five seconds, and Francis Coppola's *Tetro* (2009) is five seconds. Action films on average get down to, over the course of a whole film, three-and-a-half seconds per shot. You can also compare two films shot within a year of each other: *Sunset Boulevard* (1950), Billy Wilder's film, and The Third Man (1949). By today's standards, *Sunset Boulevard* is slow in terms of its cutting pace; it doesn't make it any less of a wonderful film. *The Third Man*, however, which was shot the year before - definitely looks like a film that was shot and put together today. It has that same kind of quickness of tempo. So I think it depends on the film and the sensibility of the director **(Instinct)**. The quickest film ever shot, editorially, is *Man with a Movie Camera* (1929), Dziga Vertov's film, where he does one cut every frame, and he superimposes three strains at the same time. So you're looking at just a blizzard of editing...**(Zippy Zappy Zediting)** not, obviously, throughout the whole film, but there are sections there where it's inconceivable that a film could be cut quicker than that film, which was made in the late 1920s.[10] When watching, you may want to turn the, to my mind, terrible inauthentic accompanying music off. A good exercise for novice film composers, please compose a better Score!

https://youtu.be/VkKcl2-Xc7k

N.B. Murch advocates standing up all the time while editing - it obviously works - winning a double Oscar for Best Sound & Best Film Editing for *The English Patient* (1996)

---

[10] Murch. W. Imdb https://www.imdb.com/name/nm0004555/bio?ref_=nm_ov_bio_sm (accessed 08/2019)

Colour Grading

A valuable post production advantage with editing software is the amount of atmosphere an editor can add with colour grading. As long as the shots have been lit moderately well, then an expert Colour Editor can, working alongside the director improve the look of a picture almost beyond recognition from its original.

Q. **When was the first colour film made?**

A. Technicolor was first used partially in a 1917 film *The Gulf Between* but it was not until 1928 that a whole film *The Viking* was produced in full Technicolor.

Q. **Why then did films not continue to be made in colour after that break through?**

A. The process was very expensive. Primarily though, from the days German Expressionism, lighting exceptional chiaroscuro in black and white.

The Cabinet of Dr. Caligari (1920)

Nosferatu (1922)

Sunrise (1927)

Colour was not as aesthetically pleasing. Cinematographers and the world had fallen in love with the drama that monochrome images conjured.

The preference for black and white cinematography remained, culminating with the era of film noir that started with the influence of *Citizen Kane (*1941) through the 40's into the mid 50's. Up to this point only half the films produced had been in colour, not least two great epics in the same year of 1939 *The Wizard of Oz* and *Gone with the Wind.*

Q. What caused the change to more colour in the 1950's?

A. In 1950 Kodak Eastman Colour Films for Professional Motion Pictures invented a single strip colour process that was less time consuming than Technicolor and thus cheaper. By the mid 1960's colour was the format cinemas expected their public to be viewing films in, leading to increased box-office revenue.

Q. Is black and white ever used today?

A. Yes - each year at least a handful are made. It is interesting to note that today students of film tend to be averse to watching black & white films yet when given the first opportunity to create and edit a short piece they often ask how they can turn their footage into black & white.

Spielberg's *Schindler's List* (1993) was shot in black & white except where colour separation of a little girl in red coat was created by filming that particular scene in colour then desaturating by rotoscoping each frame by hand (today it is an easy effect accessed in the effects of editing software).

The 2019 Oscar for best cinematography was awarded to Alfonso Cuaron for *Roma,* a film he also wrote, directed, and edited with his vision of it always being a black and white film. He filmed it though in colour believing he would be rewarded with more tonal quality in its conversion - he was obviously right.

Director note: if your vision is a black and white film - film in colour. This in addition to extra tonal quality gives you the option of changing your mind and keeping it in colour.

Q. What is colour grading?

A. We say film when really, we mean digital. In the digital world colour grading is now synonymous with colour correction where artful professional colourists exercise their magic with an understanding of the complexities offered by various software packages - the most recognised being Blackmagic DaVinci Resolve and FilmLight Baselight. Performing those skills with genuine linear film is a complex profession far removed from digital filmmaking that is the affordable process explored here.

Digital film shot in the uncompressed capture mode of RAW (as in raw) or LOG (logarithmic) settings uses the whole dynamic range of the sensor providing the most efficient means of storing the uncompressed images. It can be alarming to view the flat washed out look that this produces. The necessary information though is all there - gloriously detailed so that it can be brought back to life in the edit with the use of LUTS (Look Up Tables).

Then correcting exposure - colour balance etc. can begin followed by Stylizing.

Q. **What is stylizing?**

A. The final process of completing the visual atmosphere and mood by colour grading each sequence that may, with artistic licence, embellish natural colours in favour of a picture almost beyond recognition from its original.

Natural   Graded

courtesy of graphicadi.com

> **Director and actor note:** "Stylized acting and directing is to realistic acting and direction as poetry is to prose" Elia Kazan. The same sentiments can be attributed to colour grading.

See Lewis Bond's colour theory video on
Colour in Storytelling here

https://youtu.be/TR3ho0A9k2I

> **Director & Editor note:**
>
> All colours mean something on an emotional level and they can help add new visual layers to your film. For example: warm colours (such as red, yellow, or orange) wake us up and get us moving while cool colours (such as blue, green, white) have a calming effect on us.
>
> It is also essential that you learn what colours mean to various cultures and traditions around the world. For example: in Western culture, black is the colour of death (mourning). In Eastern culture, the colour of mourning is white. Here is a list of 12 of the most common colours used today.
>
> 1. RED – anger, passion, rage, desire, excitement, energy, speeding, strength, power, heat, love, aggression, danger, fire, blood, war, violence.
>
> 2. PINK – love, innocence, health, happiness, contented, romance, charming, playfulness, soft, delicate, feminine.
>
> 3. YELLOW – wisdom, knowledge, relaxation, joy, happiness, optimism, idealism, imagination, hope, sunshine, summer, dishonesty, cowardice, betrayal, jealousy, covetousness, deceit, illness, hazard.
>
> 4. ORANGE – humour, energy, balance, warmth, enthusiasm, vibrant, expansive, flamboyant.
>
> 5. GREEN – healing, soothing, perseverance, tenacity, self-awareness, proud, unchanging nature, environment, healthy, good luck, renewal, youth, vigour, spring, generosity, fertility, jealousy, inexperience, envy.
>
> 6. BLUE – faith, spirituality, contentment, loyalty, fulfilment peace, tranquillity, calm, stability, harmony, unity, trust, truth, confidence, conservatism, security, cleanliness, order, sky, water, cold, technology, depression.

7. PURPLE/VIOLET – erotic, royalty, nobility, spirituality, ceremony, mysterious, transformation, wisdom, enlightenment, cruelty, arrogance, mourning, power, sensitive, intimacy.

8. BROWN – materialistic, sensation, earth, home, outdoors, reliability, comfort, endurance, stability, simplicity.

9. BLACK – No, power, sexuality, sophistication, formality, elegance, wealth, mystery, fear, anonymity, unhappiness, depth, style, evil, sadness, remorse, anger.

10. WHITE – Yes, protection, love, reverence, purity, simplicity, cleanliness, peace, humility, precision, innocence, youth, birth, winter, snow, good, sterility, marriage (Western cultures), death (Eastern cultures), cold, clinical, sterile.

11. SILVER – riches, glamorous, distinguished, earthy, natural, sleek, elegant, high-tech.

12. GOLD – precious, riches, extravagance. warm, wealth, prosperity, grandeur.[11]

Sound Designer

Q. **What does a sound designer do?**

A. Editor Walter Murch for his work on *Apocalypse Now* (1979 coined the term "sound designer". The opening scene here shows why such a skill needed a credit...

Apocalypse

https://youtu.be/mBsMpTeQMho

Along with colleagues such as <u>Ben Burtt</u> (Pixar - Star Trek - Star War films), they elevated the art and impact of film sound to a new level. Murch established the job role as "an individual ultimately responsible for all aspects of a film's audio track, from the **dialogue** and **sound effects** recording to the **re-recording** (mix) of the final track"[12].

---

[11] Marshall. D. P (2019) Film Directing Tips http://filmdirectingtips.com/archives/157

[12] Reeves, Alex. "A Brief History of Sound Design". *Advertising Week Social Club*. Advertising Week. Archived from the original on 4 March 2016. Retrieved 13 October 2015.

As far back as 1974 Murch had established the art as the Supervising Editor - Sound Montage & Re-Recording technician for *The Conversation* (1974). Here the opening scene is another master class in sound design

https://youtu.be/i-iOM7vCfBM

The following is all part of that process...

Foley

Q. Foley?

A.

Named after Jack Foley who developed the technique.

Jack Foley (1891-1967)

The **'Psycho Shower'** sound of knife into flesh is what we call 'Foley', created on that occasion by a knife stabbing a melon. 'Foley' is essential to all films, creating a heightened reality. Often the actual sound recorded on set (known as Diegetic sound) is not enough. Good 'Foley' will add another sensory dimension to your film.

Here is a fun example of how Foley is created By Sound Ideas www.sound-ideas.com

https://youtu.be/MTkGbhu7tWM

Everything has a sound unless you are in outer space where there are no atoms and molecules in air and water for sound to vibrate through...

So make sure we hear the sound we see. A football being kicked - someone typing on a keyboard etc. Too often music is lazily substituted for these sounds, diminishing the impact of the visuals in a scene. Recording specific Foley, you will enhance your viewers' sensual experience with Foley being heard complementing the music, if there is any.

Music

The *Psycho* shower scene (1960) composed by Bernard Herrmann is now an instantly recognisable piece that will, as soon as it is heard bring to mind the sequence.

Director note:

Any sound created by a radio, music player, dialogue etc., audible in the scene is **Diegetic** sound. If it is sound added on to the scene being viewed it is known as **Non-Diegetic** sound, as is the case with the *Psycho* music because it is not shown to be coming from a radio in the scene.

If you could find someone to compose suitable music (sometimes created electronically) for your script it would be a wise solution to avoid copyright and too familiar copyright-free compositions.

N.B. speeding the music up or slowing it down can make it sound interestingly different.

Copyright music

Either buy permission to use copyrighted music or buy copyright-free music. **Do Not** use any music without permission. You will not get away with it. The least that will happen (if not taken to court) is, you'll go to view your uploaded film on YouTube finding a blank audio due to you having violated copyright.

Director note: Do not fall into the trap of putting music behind everything; smothering important **Foley** and making everything bland as I have already mentioned is to be avoided. Equally, make sure any lyric to the music is not confusing the audience's ear while dialogue is being spoken.

N.B. use only instrumental music unless the lyric is to be part of the story.

A Challenge Q & A

Planning (pre-production) Filming (production) Editing (post production)

Here is a short project: challenging you to put into practice the previous Scenes guidance to producing a short film.

When your pre-production work is complete, you might like to cast, film & edit it: adding music and Foley; having 'painted with light'; directed your actors; and thus having created plenty of atmosphere for a first viewing. Don't miss out pre- and end-titling it.

THE THREE WISE DETECTIVES

FADE IN

A_____/

ESTABLISHING MASTER SHOT

INT. POLICE INTERVIEW ROOM - NIGHT

DETECTIVE HEAR NO EVIL (OFF)
She said she left it for us to look at on the table.

DETECTIVE HEAR NO EVIL and DETECTIVE SEE NO EVIL Enter room.

B_____/
MASTER SHOT

Seeing envelope on table. They both sit close to it and each other at table.

D_____/
2 SHOT MCU

DETECTIVE HEAR NO EVIL
(opens envelope and Reads to self)

D_____/
PANNING TO SINGLE CU ON HEAR...

Guilty - full confession.

Handing over the hand-written confession.

DETECTIVE SEE NO EVIL
(Reading)

Yes - guilty. When is she coming in?

DETECTIVE HEAR NO EVIL
Any minute now.

Long pause.

DETECTIVE SEE NO EVIL
Did you hear anything?

DETECTIVE HEAR NO EVIL
No. You see anything?

DETECTIVE SEE NO EVIL
I don't think I could have done.

Pause.

DETECTIVE SEE NO EVIL
How do you think she disposed of the body?

The door opens. DETECTIVE SPEAK NO EVIL
walks in and slowly sits down.

DETECTIVE SPEAK NO EVIL
So, you have my confession.

She puts her hands together as if to be handcuffed.

I brought my tooth brush.

DETECTIVE SEE NO EVIL
Yes - but I don't think I saw anything.

DETECTIVE HEAR NO EVIL
Nor I - I don't think I heard anything.

Passing the confession to DETECTIVE SPEAK NO EVIL.

DETECTIVE SPEAK NO EVIL

Long pause.

Then I haven't spoken about it with you?

DETECTIVES SEE & HEAR nod in agreement.

DETECTIVE SPEAK NO EVIL
Thank you.

Getting a tin waste paper bin. She takes out a lighter and burns the confession.

See no evil, hear no evil, speak no evil.
The bastard's cremated!

She goes to the door.

Thanks to three wise detectives.

She takes out a toothbrush from her bag.

I won't be needing this.

She exits.

DETECTIVES SEE & HEAR go to the burning bin, pick it up, look at it.

DETECTIVE SEE NO EVIL
So now we know.

DETECTIVE HEAR NO EVIL
No evidence.

FADE OUT

I have planned it to a certain point for you, showing the method of pre-production you might find it useful to adopt for your future productions that I introduced you to with the *Actress First Time On Set* **Scene 1 Shooting Script Q & A** (pages 8–10)

1. **Create a Location Ground Plan** like the following for each sequence of your film. If your film revisited this location, then characters and camera positions may be different, so another copy of this Location Ground Plan would need to be planned drawn up.

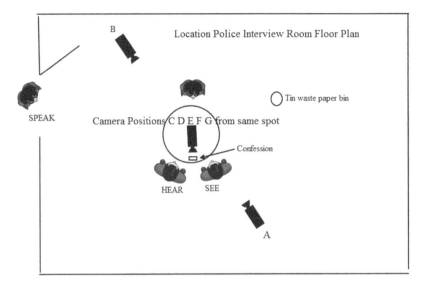

2. Design character and camera positions

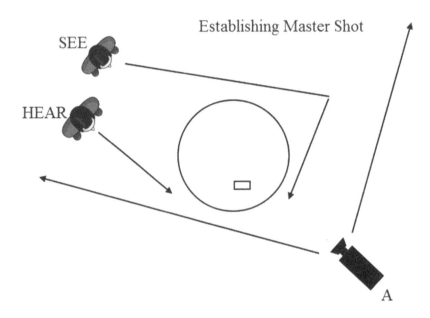

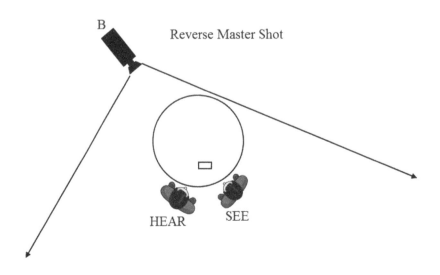

2 Shot panning to a Single Shot as each reacts

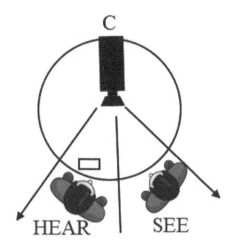

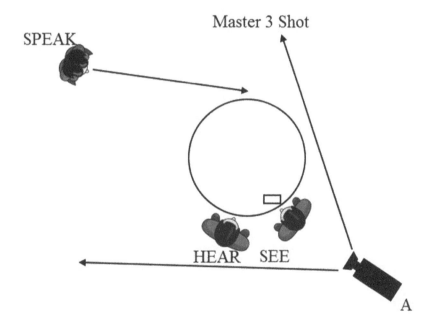

SPEAK centre of screen looking Right of camera to HEAR & Left of camera to SEE

HEAR placed centre screen looking left of camera to SPEAK & right to SEE

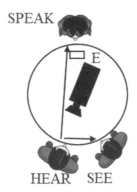

SPEAK

E

HEAR   SEE

So, to this point I have done the work for you. In previous pages I have explained the challenge of more than 2 characters in a scene. Here we have the question once again of…

Q. How can I make it look as if they are talking to each other?

A. It is partly solved with the camera positions I have designed for you **A-G**. It's all about where the eyes are looking (eye-lines)! Screen Right & Screen Left are Camera Right & Camera Left: for this exercise with camera positions **C**, **D, E, & F,** I have described the action from how you would direct the actors from their point of view.

Now, you complete the challenge using the method to make sure they are looking at each other when needed:

3. Copy the Three Wise Detectives script from the script section of the book p. 157) and download a storyboard template from www.bothsidesofthemoviecamera.film

4. Decide which camera position and shot size you would like to see for action and dialogue prior to each cut marking the script as I started to, as can be seen on the script on the previous page.

   Adopt the method there, drawing a line on the script naming the camera position **A-G** and the shot type underneath with a forward slash for cut to----------- / that may be in the middle of a line of dialogue-------- / and remember film is often 'reaction' to what we hear being said, so you could cut---------------- / away from dialogue to someone listening and reacting.

   Mark your script in the same manner throughout as you decide the shots and dialogue from the camera positions on the Location Ground Plan.

5. The storyboard will help you visualize where characters are looking and to assign dialogue. It will also help you time, pace, and appreciate how many shots the scene may be edited to. You may surprise yourself with how many shots you create for the scene.

Director note:

a/ as SPEAK leaves you might cut in the order of camera positions **A, C, B.** Camera position **C** with eye lines following her, would have to be in-between **A & B** otherwise SPEAK will suddenly be walking out screen left (A) then right (B) having broken the 180-degree line of action.

b/ make sure that actors do not jump out at the viewer by 'spiking' the camera lens

c/ you may want to insert a **P**oint **O**f **V**iew shot (POV) of the confession being cremated in the bin from either HEAR & SEE's POV or SPEAK's.

d/ it is essential to allow long pauses for reaction, allowing the text to breathe. Meaning is all in what is not said.

Alternative camera positions viewed from Establishing Shot A of all 3 characters

Character 1 looks at 2 reverse shots from positions B & C
Character 1 looks at 3 reverse shots from positions D & E
Character 3 looks at 2 reverse shots from positions F & G

Learning Lines

Many young actors that I meet seem to have no understanding of the discipline of learning text accurately. Time is not always on the actor's side for learning lines. But if it is, and a photographic memory is not in evidence, the following is an enjoyable way to learn small to very large amounts of script or even study for exams accurately!

Learning Lines for a Whole Script or Speech (the easy enjoyable way to learn)

Trust your brain!

1) It is vital that you learn the text of a script accurately as the playwright/ screenwriter has written it, word for word, paying particular attention to punctuation. It is never acceptable to improvise the playwright's/screenwriter's text. Unless of course working in a team devising.

2) Use a dictionary to find out the meaning and pronunciation of words you do not understand.

3) Read the play/screenplay in full that your speech or part are in. This will give you clues to your character. It will help you make emotional connections when remembering lines and allow you to create a believable characterization.

4) Now; familiar with your text, the fun of learning your part can begin!

   a/ Today, spend 20 minutes looking at as many lines as you feel comfortable trying to commit to memory (about 10 lines, a paragraph or page of dialogue)

   b/ After about 20 minutes, as your brain is beginning to tire of this repetition, select the following part of the text that you feel comfortable with attempting to commit to memory; start to learn that.

c/ After another 20 minutes when you begin to tire of the process completely – give yourself a break – have a cup of tea and biscuit – forget about trying to remember; take time out to relax for about 20 minutes

d/ Now – go back to learning the text you started your learning session with. Apply the same technique with the 20-minute changes for a second time, right up to the time for a second break.

e/ Take your 20-minute break as before.

f/ When you start back, this time you are not going to look at the part of text you have been learning. You are to leave that until the same time the following day – when you will apply exactly the same process you have been practising today.

g/ And then after your following day's practice you leave the part of text you have been learning until the same time a week later!

h/ Now today you continue learning the text from where you had your last break following the same routine until you have had enough of learning for the day.

5) This way you are giving the same amount of time to all of the text and not panicking your brain worrying about how slowly you are learning your lines. You will become familiar with the whole text, equally well. Learning will start to be fun! Your brain will be egging you on to learn the next bit, then the next bit, then the next bit. Your brain and you will not get bored or frustrated or intimidated by the amount to learn – your brain will be excited to learn more!

6) A week later; you start working through your role, speaking the lines out loud following the same process as in the previous week. Only work on that part of the text that you were working on at the specific time in the past week.

7) You will be surprised by how much your mind has sorted the lines out in the time you have not looked at the text, and at how stimulating the learning process is becoming.

8) Work through the day and week catching up with where you were in the text at about the same time and day in the previous week allotting the same time and process. Don't forget to follow the following day process before leaving possibly for another week if you feel that is what you need.

9) You will now begin to know all of the text equally well. The lines will begin to flow. You will know the end of your part as well as you know the beginning and middle.

10) Now you can enjoy the freedom of becoming secure with an accurate memory of the text; freedom that will now allow you to take risks – experiment with line readings – characterization – and take direction!

You will now have given yourself the opportunity creatively, to develop a true interpretation of your character leading to an engaging performance.

Mirror Up To Nature

The heretic's eye view of acting theory
for
Directors and Actors
Know the Lines - Don't Bump into the Camera and Lights

The late American comedian George Burns joked "Great acting requires truth, passion, and realism. If you can fake those, you've got it made".

The pursuit of truth and realism in acting has led to a lot of theories on how to achieve its reality in performance. It is where, in my and others' opinion, a great deal of time is wasted in the classroom and workshops searching for the holy grail of how to act. It is an excellent way to occupy students, spending endless time discussing and emoting childhood memories but it delays the real work that is needed, that of working on texts, learning lines, voice work, taking direction and performing.

To take us away from the dogmatism of theory, I would like you to consider the views of two of America's leading screen & stage acting practitioners and one leading English director whose opinions reclaim the actor's craft minus the theory.

Firstly, Harold Guskin, who is an actor, director, and New York City acting coach who has taught for over thirty years many grateful stars. These include Kevin Kline, Glen Close, James Gandolfini and Bruce Willis, to name but a few. In his book 'How To Stop Acting' with a foreword by the English actor David Suchet, he states…

> when I rejected analysis and technique, I found that my imagination was free, full, and available to me again, and surprisingly, so were my emotions without prolonged work on emotional recall.[13]

---

[13] GUSKIN.H. (2003) How To Stop Acting. Faber & Faber. 2004 p.39.

'Emotional recall' being a major part of Stanislavsky's (1863 – 1938) theory of acting 'system', where it is called 'emotional memory'. Stanislavsky's 'system' is now known in Britain and America as The Method having first been introduced by "…two of his protégés Michael Chekov (1891 – 1955) and Richard Boleslavsky (1889 – 1937), and subsequently adapted to the American actor by Lee Strasberg (1901 – 1982) and other members of the Group Theatre in 1931…".[14] It is Lee Strasberg who is known as the father of The Method and it is at this point in America's theatrical history that Jerzy Grotowski disparagingly states that Stanislavsky has been "…assassinated after death by the vast number of those seeking to crystallize the stages of his research into the perfect prescription for achieving results."[15].

Stanislavsky was always questioning his work with "…permanent self-reform…"[16]. Since his death actors have been trained (perhaps more accurately – brainwashed) to adopt his system that had been developed into The Method by Lee Strasberg. Strasberg's contribution has been to create psycho-dramatic improvisation that feeds off 'emotional memory'. Consequently, actors attend workshops with drama teachers where more appropriately the workshop leader should be a psychiatrist. Kenneth Tynan was writing as long ago as 1961 about a production he saw at the Moscow Art Theatre "…This is Stanislavsky without Freud; physiological acting without the psychiatric glosses, beloved of so many American 'Method' actors…".[17].

So as far back as the 1950's American actors were being imbued with pseudo psychology misleadingly inspired by Stanislavsky's hijacked 'system' under the guise of The Method'. Now is the time I hope for The Method to lose its foothold on actor training. As Guskin states in his book.

Stanislavsky formulated his ideas about acting in the late nineteenth century, when Chekov, Dostoyevsky, and Strindberg were writing… he developed his 'special technique' in reaction to the general acting style of his day, which was all elegant movement, elocution, and overly dramatic displays of characters emotions that bore not a touch of truthfulness…but we are not the children of Stanislavsky's theatre, and as contemporary actors and audiences, we take it for granted that acting should be real and natural.[18]

---

[14] ROOSE EVANS, James (1991) Experimental theatre, p.6. Routledge. London.
[15] KUMIEGA, J, (1985) The Theatre Of Grotowski. p.110. Methuen.London.
[16] Ibid
[17] TYNAN, K. (1961) Curtains. Longmans, green, London, and Atheneum, New York. p.21
[18] GUSKIN.H. (2004) How To Stop Acting. Faber & Faber. 2004. p.38.

Interestingly the two protégés of Stanislavsky mentioned formerly who introduced his system to America had already broken away from Stanislavsky's Moscow Arts Theatre in search of a more **theatrical form** than the **natural style** 'the system' was producing.

So what does Guskin suggest should be put in The Method's place? Well, simply, spontaneity. In his book he talks about creating character "...the character is simply the actor's continual response to the author's lines, an on-going exploration that remains completely personal for him, from first reading through final performance". [19] This requires spontaneity and a freedom to be able to "...be continually exploring the role by freely responding to the dialogue before rehearsal, in rehearsal, and, - I know this is a controversial notion – throughout his performance on stage or film".[20] Indeed, to many directors and productions this could cause a threat to the status quo. However, 'controversial' as it may be, a genuinely intuitive and gifted actor needs this freedom to be able to live on the edge of the text, tempting the audience in all directions as the moment inspires. This is what makes the gifted actor, magnetically, excitingly dangerous, to watch. As Guskin says "we have to respond personally to the script with whatever comes, no matter how foolish it is to others or even to us. The only rule is you must never physically hurt another actor or act out a physically threatening way that enters into the other actor/s space".[21]

This freedom to appear foolish in exploration of character is absolutely essential. The rehearsal should be a time when an actor can feel free to make an absolute fool of themselves - even appear miscast. Of course, with all the actors exploring their text in this way, bedlam could ensue. It is for this reason that the objective eye of a director is needed to appropriate the wheat from the chaff. That he will have plenty of wheat to choose from will be a direct result of the freedom he has created in the rehearsal room or on the film set. Guskin is renowned for his guidance to many of the aforementioned actors, who approached him with the script of their latest movie or stage play. Obviously experienced actors feel the need for this one to one guidance prior to production rehearsals. How their directors feel is not mentioned, if indeed they have been aware of Guskin's enormous input into their finished products over the years often leading to awards for these stellar students. Perhaps it is an indictment of the all-powerful director in film, TV and theatre that actors as famous as Jane Fonda, Peter Fonda, Bruce Willis et al should have to gain their courage to try new approaches to a text away from the homogenous

---

[19] Ibid. p.48.
[20] Ibid. pp 41-42.
[21] Ibid. p 51.

creative process of production. If they did know I can hear the cry of 'Oh – I see Guskin has got at you again'. Well personally as a director, I would prefer to have to say that than to hear an actor ask "As this vegetable character I'm playing, of the Tomato, what is my motivation to sit?' as Dustin Hofman's actor character in *Tootsie* (1982)inquired. The Guskin actor would have been offering plenty of 'spontaneous' choices for the director as the Tomato. Alfred Hitchcock's reply when asked the same question was 'your character's in the script, motivation your salary'.

Secondly, we come to the great writer/director and sometime actor David Mamet. His book 'True and False' is delightfully subtitled 'Heresy and Common Sense for the Actor'. David Mamet has penned among many stage and screen successes 'Glengarry Glen Ross' (for which he won the Pulitzer Prize) and 'Oleanna'. He is a great playwright/screenwriter. So, to read from him

> the only reason to rehearse a play is to learn to perform the play …it is not to "explore the meaning of the play"- the play, for the actor, *has* no meaning beyond its performance. It is not to "investigate the life of the character." There are just lines on the page.[22]

To read this from a playwright who can only want the best for his text in performance should be liberating for all actors exhausting themselves with The Method and other like-minded theories for performance.

David Mamet has had bad experiences of actors reading too much into his written text. The actor buries himself beneath a subtext of 'emotional memory' to the detriment of communicating the lines the playwright has written. Sanford Meisner[23] (1905 – 1997) a founder actor-director member of the group theatre in 1931 with Lee Strasburg, later at the time of its disbandment in 1939 remarked that "Actors are not guinea pigs to be manipulated, dissected, let alone in a purely negative way. Our approach was not organic, that is to say not healthy."[24] However this did not stop him from developing his own 'Meisner Technique' once again based on Stanislavsky and leaving in his wake a Meisner Academy, a centre for the training of actors. Alarmingly to David Mamet, Meisner later stated

> it takes 20 years to become an actor. It does not guarantee stardom or an agent or even a living. You must be excited about the work and still feel the thrill go up your spine when you read "The Collected Works" of …Lee Strasberg's "Dream of Passion", "Stella Adler On Ibsen, Strindberg and Chekhov", …

---

[22] MAMET, D. (1999) True & False. Vintage Books. Mamet. 1998. p.52.
[23] http://www.themeisnercenter.com/meisnerBio.html
[24] Ibid

The Life and Work of Konstantin Stanislavsky,.. It is the blood that pumps throughout your veins...[25].

Of course, 'excitement' and 'thrill' are essential for the dedication and passion that being a successful actor requires. This is all possible though, without the brow beating analysis and self-introspection that those who train actors often inculcate. Mamet is scathing about this 'paint by numbers' preoccupation with playmaking.

A play can be rehearsed quickly, by a group of competent actors who know the lines, and are prepared, with the help of the director, to find the simple actions associated with them and to be arranged into an appropriate stage picture. If this is so, why squander months in rehearsal and years in school? The reason is economic'.[26]

This complication of what really is a simple craft if genuine talent resides in an actor has been an obfuscation that benefits the economic and statistical life of institutions that run drama training courses. The indoctrination of theory that produces

> The paint-by-number mechanical actor...judging himself and his performance constantly... by preordained checklist...so the audience is robbed of any immediacy, and intimacy, of the unforeseen, of those few things, in short, those sole things capable of rendering a performance of a play superior to a reading of the text.[27]

Mamet himself teaches promulgating scathingly that

> The paint – by – numbers analysis of emotion memory, sense memory, character dissection, and so on, is designed for the hobbyist who can take the piece apart at her leisure with never a thought of performance. Its merit is in its potentially endless consumption of time.[28]

Of primary concern in the future of education in this area must be the text, voice production with elocution, movement and relaxation, rehearsal leading to performance. It is I think, worth noting that the Polish theatre director Jerzy Grotowski who has had a considerable influence on contemporary theatre, not only required his actors to be physically fit but also exceptionally vocally adroit. He was particularly demanding with regard to diction (elocution) "...The best training in diction is obtained in one's personal life. The actor must pay continual

---

[25]

[26] MAMET, D. (1999) True & False. Vintage Books. Mamet. 1998. p. 52.

[27] Ibid. p..54.

[28] Ibid. p54.

attention to his pronunciation, even outside the environment of his work…".[29] Most welcomingly, we can add to that, the anecdote told in Peter Barkworth's book 'About Acting' where he relates a conversation between the actors Robert Stephens, Colin Blakely and two visiting Russian Moscow Arts Theatre actors who had been trained by Stanislavsky. Blakely asks, "were there any [things that Stanislavsky said] which stand out particularly in your memory?". The two actors thought long and hard and then one said "Actually, I do remember something he often said, 'The three most important things for an actor are voice, voice and yet more voice'.[30]

The skill of acting can only be improved with the opportunity to rehearse and perform regularly with screenplay and play texts. The discipline of regularly working with a text and an audience, a text and a camera, is the only way to learn the craft of acting. It is a vocation in which actors will never feel that they know it all. There is not an actor that you can meet, no matter how long in the tooth, who will not tell the listener that they are still learning new tricks.

Many actors who are introduced to Stanislavsky, Lee Strasberg's The Method, and many other theories of acting in the quest for 'Mirror Up To Nature' realism tend to end up looking and sounding as if they are 'over thinking'.

So, thirdly, the following is some excellent advice for actors/directors from the great director Tyrone Guthrie (1900-1971) who as you will see has another term for this 'over thinking' and the same observations as Guskin and Mamet…

> **Real life is full of stagey incidents and stagey behaviour, and there is no particular merit in the sort of acting which shuns staginess, <u>unless it clearly substitutes something more interesting and moving. This is what 'method' acting rarely does</u>. Too often it produces tiny manifestation which appear to be symptoms of constipation rather than any recognisable emotion.** This is not because 'The Method' is wrong. It is because too often its practitioners attempt to apply amateur psychoanalysis and then to express the result with inadequate technical means. There is no great point, so it seems to me, in an actor having splendid, original and pure ideas which they have never learned to express: no point in having 'know what' unless they have adequate 'know how'.[31]

'…Stagey incidents and stagey behaviour…'? I hear 'The Method' acolyte ask. Well yes, Patrick Tucker in his seminal 'Secrets of Screen Acting'[32] points out that

---

[29] GROTOWSKI, J. (1968) *Towards A Poor Theatre*. A Methuen paperback. .p.137.

[30] BARKWORTH, P. (1980) *About Acting*. Methuen Drama. p.95.

[31] GUTHRIE, Tyrone. (1971) *Tyrone Guthrie On Acting*. Studio Vista. London.. p.78

[32] TUCKER, P. (2015) Secrets of Screen Acting. Routledge Arts.

the 'over acting part' will usually be the speaking too loudly. Finally, it needs to be acknowledged that there were many brilliant performances on screen by the likes of Cary Grant, James Stewart, Ingrid Bergman, Greta Garbo, Katherine Hepburn, Humphrey Bogart, Vivien Leigh, Joan Fontaine, Bette Davis, Hattie McDaniel, Sidney Poitier, Spencer Tracy, Laurence Olivier et al from before the famed Actors' Studios influence took hold. There is no better example than 'It's a Wonderful Life' made in 1946 with a very large cast including James Stewart, Donna Reed, Henry Warner, Lionel Barrymore, Henry Travers, all giving supreme screen performances.

I suggest, that still, today, the most valuable training an actor should acquire is voice production. They need to learn how to neutralise any accent they may have, thus becoming a vocal blank canvas, that will allow a variety of characters they are cast in, to be painted on it, freeing their imaginations to create for each character an individual voice to speak with. David Suchet & Meryl Streep are great examples of actors who have done just that with the variety of roles they have played.

Actor note:

Two-time Best Actress Oscar winner Elizabeth Taylor

"When you are doing a part, you have to blank everybody on the set other than the actor you are opposite - the camera included - you have to be aware of where it is - because there is a kind of 'umbilical cord' between you and the camera.

I'm purely an 'instinctive actress'. There are method actors and method actors. Some that have to stand in the corner and shake their hands - jump up and down until they get what they call the line - and I find that I have a hard time being patient with that - either you know when you do the scene what your line is and you should know before you start to film what direction you are going in - you shouldn't do it 5 minutes before a take and then decide which way you are going - I think you should know before hand - I prepare in my head so it gets from my head to my heart and I know what I'm meaning - then you do it on the set and that's when you 'become'. I can switch from being myself into character in a matter of seconds - because I do, like a mental 'snap' and I can 'become' Martha in *Who's Afraid of Virginia Woolf?* (1966 2nd time Best Actress Oscar winner) and do it just for the length of the take - and when they say cut - drop it - and usually go into a joke to get out of it". (*Elizabeth Taylor Interview 1981 South Bank Show, Sky Arts*)

Scene 9

Screenplays

Original Short Film Screenplays to Make, Adapt or
Workshop Film Acting Techniques

with

mostly small casts, that for many allow for; colour blind casting;
male/female; same sex casting options

The American crime author and screenwriter Jim Thompson amusingly stated, 'There is only one plot - things are not what they seem'. The '...not what they seem ...' part, of course requires a writer's imagination, without it no story would exist. It always seems to me, to be a severe anomaly by the film industry that they do not put the screenwriter's name above the title. Posthumously William Shakespeare usually gets such billing. We can thoroughly enjoy a film, be able to name its stars and possibly the director, but seldom the screenwriter, without whom our escapism could not have happened.

Screenplays can go through many drafts and often this can mean a change of screenwriter. Screenwriter William Goldman (*The Princess Bride*, *Butch Cassidy and the Sundance Kid*, *All The President's Men*, *Misery* and many more) had the ending of his film *Marathon Man* rewritten by the equally famous screenwriter Robert Towne (*Shampoo*, *The Last Detail*, *Mission Impossible* 1 & 2 etc.,) who in turn had the ending of his Oscar-winning original screenplay *Chinatown (1974)* changed by his director Roman Polanski.

The life of a screenwriter is tough. Goldman has written *Adventures in the Screen Trade* and its sequel *What Lie Did I Tell?* Both are hilarious, heart-breaking, frustrating accounts of his experience at the top of his craft that are well worth reading for those who want to write.

It is not my intention here to give any instruction on writing screenplays other than to say: first find the subject/idea, then - research, research, research. Do not start writing the characters talking to each other until you have wrung the research around the subject dry. Always put yourself in your audience's position viewing it. Answer the 'what if?' scenarios, and apply, who, what, where, when, how and why does the story, do the characters, develop as they do? Is there a through line of believability. If there isn't and the characters all wake up from a dream, the audience will feel cheated and know that the screenwriter's imagination couldn't come up with an ending. The following screenplays are for rehearsing with, adapting, or in the case of some, you may feel worth trying your hand at creating a short film from, as they are.

Director and Actor note: <u>Let the dialogue breathe.</u> In film what is not spoken is as powerful as what is. Allow time for thoughts and reactions between lines. Fictional filmmaking inspires heightened reality, as with the artist and their canvas.

Actors, no 'mumbling':
<u>Consonants, tell the story - vowels, the emotion.</u>
Your screenwriter wrote dialogue to be heard.

Good Luck

N.B. if used please acknowledge **By Anthony Barnett** or **Adapted from a script/ idea by Anthony Barnett**

Take 1

Short Challenging Scripts

Trust Me

Genre: Psychological Drama

Casting: 2 – Female/Male

Filming & Acting Challenge:

This is loosely based on a real story.

The two separate locations with the other actors being able to be seen on their Face Time screens is going to be a challenge directorially.

Plenty of POV's to the screens.

Jenny's fear is real and her only protection is Paul. All the time she is fishing for him to reassure her of it.

That she realizes at the end he is not who she has thought he is – will break hers and our, the audience's, hearts.

Additional possibility:

The screenplay could start with a montage of them together with Jane being waved off at the station back to university.

FADE IN

INT. PAUL'S BEDROOM – NIGHT

PAUL is talking on FACE TIME to JENNY who we see speaking from his ipad that is propped up beside him while he works on his laptop

> JENNY ON SCREEN
> I'm telling you. Someone came to my room here in
> the halls of residence because they had found my
> picture online advertising me as a hooker!

INT. JENNY'S UNIVERSITY ROOM – NIGHT

JENNY's ipad on her bedside table with PAUL on screen. She is sitting up in bed with pen, writing pad and a couple of books she is studying with.

PAUL ON SCREEN
What did you do?

JENNY
What did I do? I called university security of course!
What do you think I did? Open my legs?

INT. PAUL'S BEDROOM – NIGHT

JENNY ON SCREEN
I'm telling you Paul. I'm being cyber stalked. Someone
must have hacked our accounts. Those pictures you
took of me in the bath. They've not only been sent to
friends including those on my course but worse – my
Dad! They must have been sent to you.

INT. JENNY'S UNIVERSITY ROOM – NIGHT

PAUL ON SCREEN
Yes – they were – I thought it was you sending them
because you were missing me.

JENNY
I miss you. Help me. Please help me Paul.

PAUL ON SCREEN
Your Dad got them?

JENNY
Yes my Dad got them –

INT. PAUL'S BEDROOM – NIGHT

JENNY ON SCREEN
- and worse Paul – he thought it must be you.

PAUL
What!?

JENNY ON SCREEN
I know. He's just trying to protect me. You were his
obvious target.

INT. JENNY'S UNIVERSITY ROOM – NIGHT

PAUL ON SCREEN

He and your Mum have never liked me.

INT. PAUL'S BEDROOM – NIGHT

JENNY ON SCREEN

This isn't about you!

INT. JENNY'S UNIVERSITY ROOM – NIGHT

PAUL ON SCREEN

I know – I know. I'd probably think the same. But you don't do you?

INT. PAUL'S BEDROOM – NIGHT

JENNY ON SCREEN

Of course not. Paul help me – who could be doing this? I love you –

(Starting to cry)

PAUL

I love you.

We see PAUL on his laptop and cut to its screen and see an image of JENNY with wet hair hands seductively stroking through it, designed as an advert. He types underneath 'I'M WET FOR YOU – CALL ME (M) 0161 27892'

He presses 'Send'.

Whilst he has been doing the above he has been saying

PAUL

Come back this weekend. I'll protect you. I'll track down whoever is doing this to you. Trust Me.

JENNY ON SCREEN

Oh Paul – what would I do without you? You make me feel so safe. Just talking to you is so good. Can't wait to be with you.

INT. JENNY'S UNIVERSITY ROOM – NIGHT

JENNY puts books on her side table

> JENNY
> Lets keep this on while we go to sleep.

She tucks herself in leaving the light on.
> Night lover.

Long Pause.

> PAUL ON SCREEN
> (Coldly)
>
> I wish your Mum and Dad hadn't persuaded you to
> abort our baby.

INT. PAUL'S BEDROOM – NIGHT

PAUL switches FACE TIME OFF.

INT. JENNY'S UNIVERSITY ROOM – NIGHT

> JENNY
> What?

Sitting up grabbing ipad seeing screen is blank.
> What? Paul?
>
> (Realisation – it couldn't be could it? Screaming out
> with the agony of the thought breaking down)
> No !!!!!!!!!! Dad's right...No!!!!!!

She grabs her phone. Dials 101
> Police...

FADE OUT

Oh -Dear -ITIS

Genre: Absurdest Comic

Casting: 2 – Male/Male – Female/Female – Female/Male

Filming & Acting Challenge:

Comedy is the hardest art form to achieve. It is easy to make an audience cry – but to cry with laughter, well, there is the true skill. This always causes me to rail at the world of film who too rarely seem to recognize comic film actors with Oscars.

This script requires good likeable comedy actors with that old requisite chemistry between them. It will be their ability to play the script for real with eccentric characterizations that may lead to winning that rare comic recognition.

Directing comedy is an equal challenge. The camera has to be where the audience needs to see the reactions. An ability to edit the piece with the correct pace will make or break the performances.

Comedy requires plenty of High Key Lighting.

N.B. Having travelled performing in comedies it was noticeable at different theatres each week, that where the lighting set-up was dimmer than usual, the laughs were less.

Plus: try adding some canned laughter in the edit as an experiment.

FADE IN

INT. DOCTORS SURGERY – DAY

DOCTOR sits by his desk and computer. Knock at the door.

                    DOCTOR
          Come in.

PATIENT enters

                    PATIENT
          Hello doctor. I've come for a general medical check
          up for a life insurance.

Sits down.

DOCTOR

Yes – right. You seem a little out of breath.

PATIENT

No – I feel fine.

DOCTOR

You look a bit pale.

PATIENT

Never felt better.

DOCTOR

Are you sure?

PATIENT

yes.

DOCTOR

That could be a sign of 'over- confident-itis'.

PATIENT

'Over-confident-itis'?

DOCTOR

Yes – you think all is well, but oh dear.

PATIENT

Oh dear?

DOCTOR

Yes – 'oh-dear-itis'.

PATIENT

'Oh-dear-itis'?

DOCTOR

How do you feel now?

PATIENT

Well..

DOCTOR

You see 'over-confident-itis'.

PATIENT

No – I meant – well – I'm not sure how I feel now.

DOCTOR

Ah that's better. How do you sleep?

PATIENT

With my eyes shut.

DOCTOR

Ha Ha Ha very funny!

PATIENT

No – I do – with them shut.

DOCTOR

I see. So you also suffer from 'no- sense-of humour-itis'.

PATIENT

Am I dying?

DOCTOR

Yes most probably – for a laugh!

PATIENT

When I came in here I felt fine, now I'm depressed.

DOCTOR

You should cut down on drinks.

PATIENT

I don't touch a drop.

DOCTOR

You should cut down on smoking.

PATIENT

I don't smoke.

DOCTOR

You should stop taking drugs.

PATIENT

I don't do drugs.

DOCTOR

You should cut down on sex.

PATIENT

Haven't had sex in ages.

DOCTOR

In that case. Here's your

prescription. Get yourself a drink, learn to smoke, do some drugs, and find a partner for plenty of sex.

DOCTOR

Have you a next of kin?

PATIENT

No.

DOCTOR

Then to conclude. Make me a beneficiary of your will and you will have passed this medical for your life insurance with flying colors.

Congratulations. Feeling better?

FADE OUT

Pretty Woman

Genre: Drama

Casting: 2 – Male/Male

Filming & Acting Challenge:

There is nothing pleasant about these characters although they are obviously not stupid by their style of dialogue. The drunken drama of the scene does not excuse their behaviour.

Directing this, the feel of a nightclub atmosphere has to be prevalent.

The POV of the girl's purse with credit cards and money has to be clear for the audience to see with an identity card with a picture of the girl (Pretty Woman).

Possible Addition:

Clubber comes into the toilets. They drop the purse and cards in the basin taking the cash and exit. The person who came in, after having a pee, goes to wash his hands , sees what is in the basin, picks up purse and credit cards...

as a bouncer comes in and catches him red handed.

FADE IN:

INT. NIGHTCLUB TOILET – NIGHT

MUSIC can be heard from the dance floor in the background. We see Male Characters A & B drunkenly fighting.

> A
> Stop...Stop...she's not worth it. Both break off from
> fight

> B
> Pretty woman...worth it to me.

Character A Gets some toilet paper for a bloodied nose. Hands a clothes brush to B to dust himself down.

A

We are fighting because we're reproductively focused.

B

(slowly drunkenly understanding what A meant)

Yeah...right on! And my knob wants to be the winner

A

Anyway... she wouldn't be interested in either of us.

B

Oh yeah? Why not?

A

We're not wealthy... and we are not kind. Two attributes all women look for.

B

You and your psychobabble... Who said we're not wealthy?

Character B pulls out a woman's purse from his inside pocket and starts to look at credit cards and identity card of girl (Pretty Woman) and count money.

A

Well we're certainly not kind!

They both break into laughter at their ill gotten-gain.

FADE OUT.

Stick Up

Genre: Drama

Casting: 2 either sex

Filming & Acting challenge: find a location away from a busy main road. The 'stick' needs to be a good solid pencil width twig about 25cm.

Director give yourself plenty of time to get 'coverage' – 'reaction shots'.

Actors – it's what's <u>not said</u> between the lines that matters the most (thought – reaction).

FADE IN

EXT. SUBURBAN STREET – DAY

We see character 'A', a person obviously down on their luck walking aimlessly past character 'B', a person attending their garden. Within a split second character 'A' picks up a stick and holds it to character 'B's back.

A

Don't move – there's a gun at your back.

Now – if you give me your money I'll not shoot.

but if you don't give me your money – if you have any – I'll not shoot. I don't want to go to prison if I didn't get anything out of it.

So either way you're not going to get shot.

So there's no reason to give me your money is there?

Oh I'm no good at this – help?

'B' turns around to confront the assailant

B
(in threatening manner)

Desperate times for desperate measures.

Picking up garden shears that they have been gardening with and were left open.

'A' offers the 'stick' in desperation to appease the danger of the shears pointing in their direction.

> You're right, it wouldn't have been
> worth shooting me for...

Taking out a £20 pound note from pocket and holding it out

> this...

Pause.

> It's yours

'B' takes the stick. 'A' takes the money.

> I hope you now have a better day.

FADE OUT

Men

Genre: Comedy

Casting: 2 – Female/Female

Filming & Acting Challenge:

This is a piece to practise continuity and comedy acting with.

Get your actors to mark their scripts at what point they are to pour wine and what word they are going to drink on. If that is done then all shots should blend nicely for continuity.

The actors need to be cheekily relaxed and not inhibited. Film it through as a Master Shot.

Then the fun for continuity can begin with the reverse shots of a Medium Close Up and Close Up.

Make sure you do not cross the line by,seeing that, in the reverses one character is Screen Left Looking Right with the other Right of Screen looking Left.

You may want to try and fit a POV shot into a wine glass so as an audience we can wish we were drinking too!

FADE IN:

INT. WINE BAR. DAY

Girl chat. Female characters A & B sit at a table. Wine bottle between them and drinking from glasses.

A
Why do some men claim to be sexual athletes?

B
Because they always come first!
(Both laugh)

A

Oh you are funny...Do you ever talk to him when you're...you Know

(indicates making love)

B

Only if he telephones!

(Once again both roar with tipsy laughter)

A

We...we...love em really...Hey...mine walked 3 miles the other day in the rain because the car had broken down in the middle of nowhere and neither of us had our phones on us.

B

Yeah... Well that's what they are designed for

A

Yeah ...and when he came back dripping wet I said 'what took you so long'.

B & A

That's what we're designed for!

(Both laugh hysterically)

FADE OUT.

Plastic Relationship

Genre: Drama

Casting: – 2 – Male (non speaking) – Female (Female showreel piece)

Filming & Acting Challenge:

This is a short but challenging piece to get right. The bar atmosphere needs to be real.

Find a location with a bar. Make sure it is a quiet time. Piped music will need to be turned off. Be aware of noisy fridges and air conditioning.

The actress will need the voice over lines to be read out loud to her off screen while being filmed 'reacting'.

Director make sure you get her to react visibly to what she is thinking.

If tears cannot be produced on the hundredth take at the end use Glycerine!

Lights will need to be concealed as well as camera from the obvious fun you can have getting mirror shots.

Continuity with the mixing of the cocktail and £50 note and change with accompanying Foley will need choreographing.

The POV of cuts on her wrist with the sleeve of her blouse being pulled down to cover them will need to be worked out skilfully. It will need to edit in with her and the man's reaction shots.

MUSIC CAN BE USED SUBTLY TO INTENSIFY HER FINAL BREAKDOWN.

FADE IN:

INT. BAR – DAY

A young BARMAID is serving a respectable MAN. As she is getting a shot of Vodka from an optic to make a cocktail her MOBILE RINGS Answering the phone

BARMAID

I can't talk now – I'm at work

She terminates the call and puts the phone down. As she continues to make the cocktail we hear in VOICE OVER

> BARMAID (V.O.)
> Yeah – work – always at work – what is it you said? 'A woman's work is never done – that's why we get paid less'- and what are you doing at the moment? Scanning the job pages? No – checking up on me to make sure I'm at work.

Passing cocktail to man

> BARMAID
> That'll be £7.80 please

> BARMAID (V.O.)
> Why can't you be like him? – smart – professional...

MAN hands £50 note to her

> BARMAID (V.O.)
> Wealthy...

As she receives the cash her sleeve pulls up to reveal self harm cuts on her upper wrist

> BARMAID (V.O.)
> Oh God – did he see ?

> BARMAID
> (to MAN embarrassed)

> Cut myself – not deliberately – getting plastic flowers out of a glass vase I knocked over – glass everywhere...

> She checks £50 note to make sure its original then gets change while speaking the following

> BARMAID
> Though some people do – self harm – not me – how could anyone put themselves through that pain?

Handing the change

: noneoping

BARMAID

What do you do then? I mean when not listening to some ditzy Barwoman excusing her accident- prone adventures...no let me guess – you're a psychiatrist specializing in dysfunctional behavior

(she over compensates with embarrassed giggles) The MAN acknowledges her with an expression implying that she may be right. BARMAID looks at her wrist again

BARMAID
(giggles turn to crying)

Plastic Flowers – Plastic Relationship!

FADE TO BLACK

BARMAID

What do you do then? I mean when not listening to some ditzy Barwoman excusing her accident- prone adventures...no let me guess – you're a psychiatrist specializing in dysfunctional behavior

(she over compensates with embarrassed giggles) The MAN acknowledges her with an expression implying that she may be right. BARMAID looks at her wrist again

BARMAID
(giggles turn to crying)

Plastic Flowers – Plastic Relationship!

FADE TO BLACK

Shit the Bed

Genre: Ethereal Mystery

Casting: 2 – Male/Female – several extras

Filming & Acting Challenge:

Directing skill and patience will be exercised here.

A split-screen effect is needed towards the end showing the same character interacting with their dead and alive self. This will be a challenge for continuity including that of lighting.

This is a vibrant club with all extras dancing around. The camera has to take us on the trip that the Young Man is on. The audience need to realize what has happened at the same time he does.

Sound: the club music can be played to get the extras and cast moving to the beat but it needs to be turned off for the dialogue and edited in later. Otherwise editing will be a nightmare – be warned!

Lighting: clever lighting has to make the Girl look Angelic.

FADE IN

INT. RAVE – NIGHT

We see a YOUNG MAN dancing inanely around a beautiful GIRL in a Bright white light. The MUSIC is House, Big Beat, Electro, Ecstasy Driven Music.

> YOUNG MAN
> Oh Man! Good 'E' Eh? Goody!, Good 'E'! I dig
> your wings.
>
> Did it hurt when you fell from heaven? You're too
> beautiful for this place. Fancy coming back to mine?

> GIRL
> It's your turn to come to mine.

YOUNG MAN

Whoa hay! Of course. Janice. God I loved you. You look so different Jan. Man, I heard you had OD'd a couple of years back. Can it really be? Wow! How could I have ever let you get away. I'm yours. Lets get to your place. O Man!

GIRL

It's your time.

YOUNG MAN

Yeah! My time. Your Time. Anytime anyplace. Woohoo lets go! Cloud Nine.

He starts to go but is frozen to a stop by the sight of himself being carried out from the dance area. Everyone stands watching. The music stops. Silence. We hear girls weeping. Quietly MUSIC starts to play again melding a mix of classical extraordinary heavenly music with the Ecstasy Driven Music.

Clever trick Man. Hey that looks like me.

GIRL

It is.

YOUNG MAN

He is Dead. Molly? Oh Man what a high. Funny. Funny. Funny.

GIRL

It's your time.

YOUNG MAN

You're so beautiful. He is dead.

GIRL

You are dead.

YOUNG MAN

You are dead?

GIRL

Yes we are dead.

YOUNG MAN

I am dead? Oh Man. Shit the bed!

FADE OUT

The Three Wise Detectives

Genre: Drama

Casting: 2 Male – 1 Female

Filming & Acting Challenge: It is all in the reactions, pauses and subtle action. What is not said and what lies behind the dialogue. Why would the Detectives want to let their colleague off a crime? I know why: can you get the audience to think the same?

Prop: waste paper bin must be metal or some other safe receptical to withstand burning. Make sure **Health & Safety** is observed with a **fire extinguisher** near-by and be careful of setting off smoke detectors. Get permission so that if there is a detector security can isolate it knowingly for a short period of time.

Possible Additions: Shot of Exterior of Police station, setting the scene.

FADE IN

INT. POLICE INTERVIEW ROOM – NIGHT

DETECTIVE HEAR NO EVIL (OFF)
She said she left it for us to look at on the table.

DETECTIVE HEAR NO EVIL and DETECTIVE SEE NO EVIL Enter room. Seeing envelope on table. They both sit close to it and each other at table.

DETECTIVE HEAR NO EVIL
(opens envelope and Reads to self)

Guilty – full confession.

Handing over the hand written confession.

DETECTIVE SEE NO EVIL
(Reading)

Yes – guilty. When is she coming in?

DETECTIVE HEAR NO EVIL
Any minute now.

Long pause.

DETECTIVE SEE NO EVIL

Did you hear anything?

DETECTIVE HEAR NO EVIL

No. You see anything?

Pause.

DETECTIVE SEE NO EVIL

I don't think I could have done.

How do you think she disposed of the body?

The door opens. DETECTIVE SPEAK NO EVIL walks in and slowly sits down.

DETECTIVE SPEAK NO EVIL

So, you have my confession.

She puts her hands together as if to be handcuffed.

I brought my tooth brush.

DETECTIVE SEE NO EVIL

Yes – but I don't think I saw anything.

DETECTIVE HEAR NO EVIL

Nor I – I don't think I heard anything.

Passing the confession to DETECTIVE SPEAK NO EVIL.

DETECTIVE SPEAK NO EVIL

Long pause.

Then I haven't spoken about it with you?

DEECTIVES SEE & HEAR nod in agreement.

DETECTIVE SPEAK NO EVIL

Thank you.

Getting a tin waste paper bin. She takes out a lighter and burns the confession.

See no evil, hear no evil, speak no evil. The bastard's cremated.

She goes to the door.

  Thanks to three wise detectives.

She takes out a toothbrush from her bag.

  I won't be needing this.

She exits.

DETECTIVES SEE & HEAR go to the burning bin, pick it up, look at it.

    DETECTIVE SEE NO EVIL
So now we know.

    DETECTIVE HEAR NO EVIL
No evidence.

        FADE OUT

The Dress

Genre: Drama

Casting: – 1 – Female (Showreel piece)

Filming & Acting Challenge:

Her friend and her are obviously both selfish judging from their behaviour towards each other.

Continuity needs to be worked out. The actress and director need to work out business that will occur at certain words in the script.

Somehow the actress has got to make us feel some compassion for her situation.

A template of a website needs to be created for the POV of what her friend has written about her.

Directing this piece – there is no need for the GIRL to be stationary. You could have her moving about her room in frustration holding her phone and glancing back at the laptop for the POV's to be inserted.

A variety of shot sizes and angles could be filmed to help add to the frustration of the GIRL'S predicament.

FADE IN:

INT. ROOM – NIGHT

GIRL speaking on mobile phone holding it in the palm of her hand while looking at laptop/ipad.

> GIRL
>
> I'm looking at stuff you've plastered about me all over the internet – No need to make an evil website about me. I didn't even fancy him. You were wearing the dress that I wanted to wear. I bought that dress first and you made me return it because it was your birthday. Well that's a nine year friendship for you. That's Why I did it – I'm not going to lie – that's why I did it...I wanted that dress so I thought I'd

sleep with your boyfriend to get back at you. You should have just let me wear the dress – it'd have been so much easier, then none of this would have happened. Like why?

She looks at webpage reading more for a moment – then.

Stop this evilness – I haven't also slept with his friend. Why did you add that? Anyway – I think I've wasted enough time on you – can you just stop spreading rumours all over Facebook, twitter and this evil webpage. I'll have to change colleges now. Thanks for ruining my life Bitch!

She terminates the call and slams the Laptop/ipad lid down.

FADE OUT.

Speed Date

Genre: Comedy

Casting: 3 – Male/Female – Off-screen Organizer (O.S)

Filming & Acting Challenge:

Can you get this date filmed in 3 minutes?

Create the environment of an authentic Speed Dating occasion.

The fun of this piece is the revelation at the end. Depending on your casting what would be the result?

Directing, the camera needs to salivate with the male and female gaze taking your audience with the seduction – or not – as the case may be!

What do males see first that is fanciable? What do females see first that is fanciable? Your camera needs to be there.

FADE IN

INT. SPEED DATING VENUE – NIGHT

JENNIFER starts to sit at a numbered table. She has a sticky label attached to her lapel with her name on it. She holds a score card and pen.

ORGANISER O.S.
Ok. You've all got your score cards. Guys and girls
you'll be ready to 'score' once the buzzer sounds.
The boys will visit each of your tables for 3 minutes
starting – now...

A BUZZER sounds and TOM with his name label and score card rushes to sit at JENNIFER's table.

TOM
I woke up laughing this morning.

JENNIFER
Were you looking under the sheets?

TOM

I'm going to like you.

JENNIFER

What isn't there to like?

TOM

You tell me.

JENNIFER

I'm high maintenance.

TOM

Then I'll be your 'Man-tenance' man.

JENNIFER

I like a man with a sense of humour.

TOM

Ha Ha ha – I'll 'Man-tain' you with my humour.

JENNIFER

No – I like a man with a sense of humour.

TOM

Sarcasm – the lowest form of wit.

JENNIFER

But the highest form of intelligence.

TOM

Jennifer...

JENNIFER

Yes Tom?

TOM

You are beautiful and intelligent.

JENNIFER

Yes Tom.

TOM

Flirtatious and sexy.

JENNIFER

Yes?

TOM

Enigmatic and gracious.

WOMAN

Tom...

TOM

Yes Jennifer?

JENNIFER

You are handsome and interesting.

TOM

Yes Jennifer.

JENNIFER

Cool and charming.

TOM

Yes?

JENNIFER

Playful and tempting.

TOM

Then eat from my tree 'Jenn-Eve-fer'.

JENNIFER

Maybe not that tempting. Remember you woke up
laughing and I don't think it would have been at one
of your puns.

The BUZZER goes off. TOM gets up.

TOM

Cut to the quick! The 3 minute quick.

He goes light-heartedly. We see each of their score cards with their speed dates
respective names on with boxes on the right side with FRIEND – SNOG –
MARRY - AVOID. We see each tick the one decided on. This will depend on how
each actor or director feels the date would have gone after the shoot – chemistry
in casting!

FADE OUT

Plagiarism

Genre: Drama

Casting: 3 – Male/Male – Female/Male – Female/Female Male/Male Female/Female

Filming & Acting Challenge:

It's all in the 'pauses' as characters suss each **other's** next moves out. Let what's not said **breathe**.

Realistic university professor's office location with a key- locking door.

The STUDENT is super cool not showing any fear when threatened.

The PROFESSOR when unmasked needs to becomes sinister enough for the audience to believe that the STUDENT is in real danger as he/she locks the door, withdrawing the key.

DJUKA in this version is a bright attractive young Serbian student.

Props: realistic well bound dissertation. Realistic looking Stuffed Pigeon.

FADE IN

INT. PROFESSOR STEPHEN HENSON'S UNIVERSITY ROOM – DAY

We see PROFESSOR STEPHEN HENSON and a STUDENT either side of a desk with the professor's name and title displayed. The student sits with his back to the door.

> PROFESSOR
> It gives me no pleasure to instigate this disciplinary
> for this act of plagiarism.

Flicking through dissertation reading

> Utilize the ionosphere – Free Energy – Perpetual
> Motion – Particle Beam "Death Ray"!

> My very words published for my doctoral degree
> 20 years ogo. How could you be so stupid as to

blatantly reproduce parts of your own professor's work.

STUDENT

Because it's not your work.

Pause

Thomas Edison restricted him because he proved to be several levels cleverer as a scientist. His invention of alternating currents and remote control signals are integrated in almost every device we use. Yet luckily for you few had heard of him; until that is to today, with his genius finally getting acknowledged. Nikola Tesla.

PROFESSOR

Where did you find his paper?

STUDENT

Same place as you.

PROFESSOR

(sarcastically)

I doubt it. The internet was in its infancy then.

My father (who was also a scientist) met Tesla where he lived in "Hotel New Yorker" shortly before he died in 1943 aged 87. The Pentagon seized all his papers which they now claim to have lost.

Holding up dissertation

The contents of this one miraculously escaped into my father's collection.

During the following The PROFESSOR gets up and walks around behind the STUDENT. We see him turn the key in the lock and withdraw it.

Sadly neither you nor I could be clever enough to have conceived its concepts.

My father left all his papers to a university library.
Since when they must have published them online
for you to find Tesla's paper.

So – aren't you lucky?

He now stands behind the STUDENT who continues to look to where he was sitting behind his desk.

I could break your neck from where I am now.

STUDENT
Painful- for you, if you get caught.

PROFESSOR
Yes – perhaps not the best 'safeguarding' practice
for either of us. But you stormed in

Shows STUDENT key.

locked the door and threatened me to let your
plagiarized work count.

STUDENT
With no gun? No knife? No fingerprints on the key?
Professor you had better keep your day job. Murder
me and you'll be caught.

PROFESSOR sits back down behind his desk. Key in hand.

PROFESSOR
Perhaps you are clever enough for a First Class
Honor's Degree then?

STUDENT
Now that's exactly what I was thinking when
I walked through that door. I also thought how cool
it would be to graduate without any debt?

PROFESSOR
Clever enough for no debt? Fifty Thousand Pounds?

Pause.

                         STUDENT
Not quite.

                         PROFESSOR
Not quite?

                         STUDENT
Not quite enough.

                         PLAGIARISM
Oh.

                         STUDENT
Rats.

                         PROFESSOR
Rats?

                         STUDENT
Rats in Tesla's hotel room.

                         PROFESSOR
                (where is he going with this)

Yes..

                         STUDENT
He had to move to another hotel
because of the complaints...

                         PROFESSOR
Yes...Trafalgar Square is plagued with
them – pigeons he loved his pigeons –
flying rats! Especially the one...

Pause.

                         STUDENT
In your draw...

.

PROFESSOR

You've done your homework

He takes out a stuffed pigeon from his desk.

INT. OUTSIDE PROFESSOR'S DOOR – DAY

We see DJUKA an attractive Serbian student with a headset listening holding her mobile.

We HEAR through her headset...

STUDENT V.O

'I had only to wish and call her and she would come flying to me'

INT. PROFESSOR STEPHEN HENSON'S UNIVERSITY ROOM – DAY

The student takes the key from the PROFESSOR and unlocks the door. In walks DJUKA. He locks it after her.

PROFESSOR

Djuka.

DJUKA

DJUKA walks flirtatiously around the back of the PROFESSOR touching him with familiarity picking up the pigeon as she does so.

PROFESSOR

Now I see – you and he...

DJUKA

See from my eyes a dying love as Tesla saw from her eyes

Indicating the pigeon

'I loved her as a man loves a women, and she loved me. As long as I had her, there was a purpose to my life'.

Here is your purpose.

She empties a bag of cocaine out of the pigeon.

PROFESSOR

Arn't you being a little dramatic.

DJUKA

Throwing the cocaine at him.

This is your purpose! I was just one of the rats you supplemented your ego with until your next fix.

PROFESSOR

He reaches across the desk picking up the pigeon.

'The bird died. At that same moment, something went out of my life and I knew my life's work was done'.

STUDENT

Now that's dramatic! Bitcoin – pay us in Bitcoin as you do your dealer.

PROFESSOR

How would you know that?

STUDENT

Handing him a piece of paper.

Recognise this Bitcoin wallet address.

PROFESSOR looks at it in recognition.

I am your dealer – Professor. It's your guarantee that you'll not hear from us again for more than we ask now.

PROFESSOR

A tooth for a tooth. An Eye for an eye. Yes – not a good idea.

So what is it to be? Two Firsts?

Opening up his computer.

Although Djuka my love, yours could well be genuine. You do have a touch of your fellow countryman's genius about you. After all, this little facade has your Serbian ingenuity all over it.

Pause.

Are you lovers?

DJUKA

She goes to the PROFESSOR draping herself over him.

Oh – a little of jealousy – I didn't know you had it in you.

Two First Class Honours, course fees for both, then not unreasonably, *enough*, for a honeymoon destination – for us both.

Professor types. STUDENT looks at his phone. There is a PING to indicate a message has been received. DJUKA goes to look over his shoulder. Excitedly rushes to the PROFESSOR putting her arms around him and giving him a kiss.

DJUKA
Thank you. Thank you.

PROFESSOR
Rates do fluctuate you know.

STUDENT unlocks the door handing the keys back to PROFESSOR. DJUKA and STUDENT start to go...

PROFESSOR
(calling after them)

Todays lesson: "what a tangled web we weave. When first we practice to deceive!".

FADE OUT

Madhatter

Genre: Absurdist Murder

Casting: 3 – Male/Male – Female

Filming & Acting Challenge:

The party props are an important part of this.

Directing it with imagination there is the opportunity to be really adventurous, possibly using slow motion in places, and dream-like tripping sound effects.

The end needs to be directed with special attention to the screen directions. If not followed it will not work. The two characters and the audience need to be made to jump out of their skins. Perhaps adding a 'death rattle' would help.

FADE IN:

INT. LIVING ROOM. NIGHT

Balloons and Party Poppers strewn about. Three mugs of tea and a Teapot on the table plus a half eaten cake. A young Woman JENNY is lying in a womb like hugging position on the floor. Male characters A & B are seated either side of the table.

> A
> Well... I thought it went very well

> B
> Yes Jenny certainly enjoyed herself.

> A
> Why did you stop going out with her?

> B
> Couldn't keep up with her...I mean look...

> A
> Yeah...she's quite something. You know when I look
> at her in that state...I sometimes think she's missing
> out on a great deal.

B

Oh Yeah...don't I know it! I mean look at me...who wouldn't want to have my babies? Pause

A

I thought it went very well.

B

The Mad Hatters Tea party!

Character A & B both laugh inanely. JENNY's body spasms turning over to reveal a cake knife thrust into her chest with blood having spread. Character A & B jump out of their skins. Then give each other a relieved congratulatory high five.

FADE OUT

Doctor Reece

Genre: Murder

Casting: 2 – Elderly Person Female/Male (non Speaking). Male/Female (Possible for Actor Showreel content)

Filming & Acting Challenge:

Although this is loosely based on a real case (that of serial male killer Dr. Shipman) I see no reason why a female doctor could not also be cast.

The Atmosphere of the end of a tiring all night A&E Hospital shift needs to be created. Hearing an ambulance siren followed by an outside shot of a Hospital could help.

It is made realistic by the fact the character begins to talk to a photo of their dead mother that has fallen from their pocket. The actor note here is to be aware of prying ears thus keeping the vocal delivery clear but quiet. Make sure the boom gets near to your actor to allow this.

A POV shot of the picture inserted several times will help the audience accept the character speaking their thoughts out loud. Make sure you do not cross the line with it. Remember screen right/screen left even with a POV of a picture.

The camera needs to let us see early on that the character is a Junior Doctor by letting us see their identity lanyard.

Likewise the camera needs to let us see a vial that says PETHIDINE clearly on it.

Macro settings on the camera will be useful for the injection shot. The trick here for the prop is to use a syringe with a sewing machine needle in it.

For the home visit film the outside of a house. Have your actor respectably dressed as a family GP would be.

Research 'The Will' document needed to make it believable. Add suitable dramatic music to suit the piece.

FADE IN

INT. HOSPITAL DOCTORS CLOAK ROOM – EARLY MORNING

A male JUNIOR DOCTOR REECE stumbles through the door in green uniform and stethoscope around his neck and name tag. He closes the door with the back of his foot with some urgency and leans his back against it. Tired and exhausted after a long nightshift he checks to see he is alone. He moves with some speed to take off his hospital attire. He fumbles to take out a pethidine vial from his jacket. He pulls out his watch with the vile. He looks at the time; it reads 6.42am – he puts the watch back holding the pethidine vial while feeling for a syringe possibly in another pocket. He notices what we saw falling from his pocket, a frayed, slightly crumpled photo that has fallen to the floor. He picks the photo up, while distractedly continuing to feel to find the syringe...

JUNIOR DOCTOR REECE

(pensively)

Looking at the photo

Hello mummy. Your 'forgiving eyes',
always forgiving -

He finds the syringe. Looking between it and the photo. –

your naughty son.

He goes to put the photo away. Stops and takes a second

longer look and then...

Nightmare, walking you to the toilet,
catheter detached, diamorphine pumping
through your veins. Exhaling in pain,
urinating blood. Horrible, horrible,
horrible shock – knowing it had
reached your kidneys. Bloody cancer!

Back to bed. Doctor increases the
dose. No more 'forgiving eyes'.
Eyeballs into the roof of your
eyelids, wide open never to shut
until, until... just the whites, your
white eyeballs stuttering in their
sockets...until, you left me mummy –
at 17. I miss you.

He puts the picture away. During the next he assembles the syringe, draws the dose from the Pethidine vial and injects himself...

> You made me feel special – are you
> proud of me? I'm now, that Doctor
> Painless, controlling the pain that
> you were eased from, as I watched
> until, until - UNTIL.
>
> I now give life or DEATH...

As the dose high hits we see

INT. LIVING ROOM – DAY

REECE now a General Practitioner. We see him administering an injection of diamorphine to an elderly patient in a chair. He sits and calmly enjoys viewing the process of the patient dying, while he drinks a cup of tea and alters the patient's will

REECE
To doctor Reece I leave... He smiles.

FADE OUT

The Experiment

Genre: Absurdist Comedy

Casting: – 2 – Female /Male

Filming & Acting Challenge:

This piece is all about fun props, a variety of interesting shots, and not least, some clever editing for synchronization of Male to Female/Female to Male voices.

Importantly this can only work if you can clearly see the mouths of each character speaking with the other's voice.

Direct your actors to have plenty of 'reaction' before speaking i.e., astonishment, frustration excitement, madness etc…,

Plenty of Foley sound could preceed this, followed by smoke, then the characters and the mise en scene becoming visible.

FADE IN:

INT. SCIENCE LAB - DAY

A scientific looking contraption is on the table with wires dangling that at sometime were attached to the… FEMALE whose lines are to be dubbed in a male voice and the MALE whose lines are to be dubbed in a female voice both seated at the table.

FEMALE

How did this happen?

MALE

I don't know.

FEMALE

I do.

MALE

How?

FEMALE

You built that contraption and attached it to the table and then to us...

MALE

Yes, and now I have proved that I can drive a car through the eye of a needle.

FEMALE

Are you mad?

MALE

You tell me!

FEMALE

No!!

FADE OUT.

Best Friends

Genre: Murder Drama

Casting: – 1 + Dead Body Actor – Female/Female – Male/Male (with change of '...I was pregnant line...').

Filming & Acting Challenge:

Your dead body actor needs to be holding a knife as if they have stabbed themselves with fingers around handle and a spill of blood.

Make sure the leading actor is wearing surgical gloves having premeditated the murder to avoid fingerprints.

If leading actor is left of screen looking right your dead body needs to be right of screen looking left obeying the 180 degree rule avoiding crossing the line. Unless that is, you are able to move the camera with a steadycam cutting back to a Master shot to show relative geographical positions.

Possible Additions: a/ you could film the murder prior to dialogue – possibly edited into slow motion with echoing screams and drowned thudding conversation. b/ the leading actor could be seen leaving the apartment and dispensing of the gloves.

FADE IN

INT. FLAT LIVING ROOM/BEDSIT – NIGHT

We see a FEMALE wearing surgical gloves finishing typing at a laptop

> FEMALE
> You had no idea and the next morning I could see
> he was confused and didn't know what to do about
> the situation

She presses print and goes to the printer

> I told him not to worry about it – that if he wanted
> to tell you he could, but if he didn't want you to
> know then I would keep it between us.

Taking paper from printer

> I was not so concerned about the consequences of you finding out to be honest, I'd get what I was given – bitchslap, hairpulling, whatever – I'd have taken it. What I was more concerned about was that where most people would just feel intense guilt I felt... almost hopeful that what happened that night was because he had feelings for me and he'd decide to tell you... But he didn't – So I had to tell you – I was pregnant –

The camera pans to a WOMAN with a bread knife sticking in her – dead – The FEMALE places the paper from the printer in a prominent position. It reads

LETTER

YOU'VE BROKEN MY HEART TOM – SLEEPING WITH MY BEST FRIEND

FEMALE

and now he'll only have me to have feelings for... best friend.

FADE OUT

Confession

Genre: Comedy

Casting: – 2 – Male/Female – Female/Female – Male/Male

Filming & Acting Challenge:

The comedy comes from playing the text for real.

a/ it is what is not said between the lines that needs to be brought out in the delivery by actors and director.

b/ the quote is from Shakespeare's Hamlet 'To Be Or Not To Be' speech.

c/ the end needs to be created for comic effect. Here the director's imagination will be shown at its most inventive.

FADE IN

INT. HOUSE – NIGHT

A young married couple A & B. B is beside bed or chair. A is in bed or chair dying...

A

Did you ask?

B

Yes

A

How long have you known?

B

I wondered if you knew and were keeping it to yourself – when they gave you 6 months...

A

I'm ready for you to tell me now. How long ?

                        B

6 months ago...

                        A

Days...

                        B

Yes

Long pause

                        A

I don't believe like you

                        B

"...the undiscovered country from whose bourn no traveller returns..." – you will

                        A

I've got a confession

                        B

You don't believe

                        A

Just in case...

Pause

I haven't always been faithful

                        B

I know

                        A

You do?

                        B

Of course – why else would I have been poisoning you?

Furious A starts to have heart failure

                              A

        I'll haunt you!

B gets up to go.

                              B
                          (smiling)

        I don't really believe

A dies.

Pause. B looks on then walks to the door. It locks. Curtains blow. Lights flicker. Items fly about the room.

                    A VOICE OVER
                  (cackling laughter)

        You'd better believe now !

                                              FADE OUT

Arthur

Genre: Whimsical Tragedy of Old Age

Casting: 2 Females

Filming & Acting Challenge:

Afternoon Tea – continuity and eating! Notice actors seldom are seen to be actually eating – usually playing with food about to eat. There is a good reason for that.

Sipping and pouring the tea will perhaps be safer options for most of the scene.

There needs to be plenty of silences so GRANDMA's thread of any memory has faded away.

Possible addition: they get up and start to go before GRANDMA stops to deliver her last line.

FADE IN

INT. TEA ROOMS – DAY

DAUGHTER-IN-LAW and GRANDMA are sitting having afternoon tea and cakes.

> GRANDMA
> You should lose some weight.

> DAUGHTER-IN-LAW
> (Amused)
>
> No – Grandma, it's because I'm pregnant.

> GRANDMA
> oh – I see. Well that's all right then.

> DAUGHTER-IN-LAW
> You're going to be a grandma again.

> GRANDMA
> I am?

DAUGHTER-IN-LAW

Do you remember your other grandchildren?

GRANDMA

No – one's going to be enough!

DAUGHTER-IN-LAW

You've already got two.

GRANDMA

Well – whatever you say dear. Is Arthur waiting in the car?

DAUGHTER-IN-LAW

We've come for a nice afternoon tea and bite to eat. Arthur is dead.

GRANDMA

Oh dear – is he – when did that happen?

DAUGHTER-IN-LAW

A couple of years ago now.

GRANDMA

Really? I used to be married to him.

DAUGHTER-IN-LAW

Yes I know – he was much loved by us all.

GRANDMA

We had a son you know.

DAUGHTER-IN-LAW

I know – I married him – John.

GRANDMA

John?

DAUGHTER-IN-LAW

He's the father of your two grandchildren and this little one to be.

GRANDMA
(laughing)

I thought you needed to lose some weight!

DAUGHTER-IN-LAW
(Laughing)

I will after its born.

GRANDMA

What?

DAUGHTER-IN-LAW

Lose weight.

GRANDMA

Yes dear – I wasn't going to mention it – but now you have –

Perhaps you shouldn't have so many of those. Is Arthur waiting in the car?

DAUGHTER-IN-LAW

No grandma – he died.

GRANDMA

Really? Oh dear that's a shame. Who got the money?

DAUGHTER-IN-LAW

John looks after it.

GRANDMA

Who got the money?

DAUGHTER-IN-LAW

John has got power of attorney.

GRANDMA

John? Do you know him?

DAUGHTER-IN-LAW

Yes I married him.

GRANDMA

Did you. Oh. Nobody tells me anything.

Did I go to the wedding?

DAUGHTER-IN-LAW

Yes- you wore a lovely dress.

GRANDMA

Arthur liked it. Is he in the car? He always waits in the car. Doesn't like shopping.

Do I know you?

DAUGHTER-IN-LAW

I'm Arthur's daughter in law.

GRANDMA

Oh – that's all right then. Have you eaten dear?

FADE OUT

Take 2
Longer
Short Challenging Scripts

Room 13

Genre: Detective

Casting: 2 – Male/Female – Female/Male (non-speaking)

Filming & Acting Challenge:

This is based on a true story that originally happened in a Paris Hotel.

Detective Roberts can be played by either a Female or Male actor. A considerable challenge to keep an audience's attention for such a long speech. Nothing new though, for this genre.

Directing this, an exterior shot of a very expensive hotel would set the scene. (Get permission and change its name if they are not happy with it being associated with the storyline).

The Male/Female actor listening to the summing up will be required to be an interesting listener. Direct them to give the camera plenty of usable reactions. Direct them to create business with appropriate props i.e., handkerchief to cry into, glasses, packing a suitcase etc.

There is no reason why this should be a static piece. The actors can be moved around.

Possible Additions:

Visuals of aspects of the summation. i.e., taking number off the door etc.,

FADE IN

INT. HOTEL ROOM – DAY

PRIVATE INVESTIGATOR ROBERTS, is summing up a missing person case to the missing person's sister

> ROBERTS
> You say you never saw your brother in his room?
> He was booked into room 13 on the first floor last
> night - you into room 25 on a floor above having
> both arrived from New York for the Edinburgh

Festival. You had a light meal together in the grill room. He retired half way through hardly able to keep his eyes open showing severe fatigue, with a headache from jet lag. You, shortly after your dessert, to your room.

You awoke at almost noon (this morning), hurriedly got yourself dressed to attend a 1 o'clock show you had booked to see with your brother. You phoned reception and asked to be put through to room 13 to hear after some silence "Madam, there is no room 13 in this hotel".

Had you mistaken the room your brother was in? You went down to speak to the receptionist who produced the hotel register with no record of your brother Paul written in it.

Seeing your distress, and as a private investigator and fellow guest, I offered you my services.

I went with you to the first floor and indeed there were rooms 12 and 14 but – appeared to be no 13.

Now I say appeared to be no 13 – I know now after further investigation there was and furthermore is a room 13!

But why hide room 13 and why erase your brother Paul's name from the register? And where is your brother?

I now have to tell you that this is a strange crime - there is deception enough to give you and your brother the right to sue.

Your brother was diagnosed with Typhoid in the night. He was delirious, phoning for help from reception. The hotel management worried that such a contagious illness could cause panic amongst the guests if they found out, so had your brother taken privately to a private isolation hospital.

The Manager chose not to inform the day staff, except for instructing a new day receptionist who was starting her first day, that there was no room 13, because of superstition.

Room 13 is to be fumigated. The night hotel maintenance man was instructed to hide its existence - information he divulged to me for a small bribe after I saw this

Taking the number 13 he found taken from the door out of his pocket.

on his (work top), with some scraps of matching first floor corridor wallpaper.

The Manager was not told by the new receptionist that you were looking for a missing brother who she thought you thought was in the fictitious room 13. Until I confronted the manager he knew nothing of a sister looking for the man from room 13 – he is deeply apologetic and tells me your brother is having the best private treatment, that the hotel will pay for, as long as you agree to keep his illness unpublicized.

My advice is for you to agree to this – here is the address of the hospital

As he takes the address from his wallet we see a cheque for £5000 from the hotel made payable to PRIVATE INVESTIGATOR ROBERTS.

FADE OUT

Urban Myth

Genre: Urban Myth

Casting: 2 – Female/Male – Male/Male – Female/Female

Filming & Acting Challenge:

This is a more instant happening based on the Urban Myth of a son brought home in a taxi, saying to the driver, he'll just go and get the fare from his Dad and when not returning, the driver goes to the door to be told the son has been dead for years. The cynics amongst us will of course think it was a family scam.

For the sake of this story we take the viewer on the journey of what if….what if the dead character really did continue as in this story.

The challenge in directing this piece is how you take the audience on the journey. The viewer needs to see the bloody violence of the character's suicide but not the character dead. So when the character is at the door the audience think well ok – perhaps the character did not hurt themselves that badly. They need to be in two minds. Perhaps this is just another unbelievable badly-made film!

The Parent in the car gets an intuition of a scream and flash of what has happened that needs to be registered with the audience.

To the Parent and the audience's relief the character is safe and at the door asking to be taken to a friend's.

Then on returning to the house the reality of the situation is revealed mysteriously to the Parent and audience.

Additional possibility:

You could have the Parent relating their experience to someone while the body is being taken away – the making of an Urban Myth.

FADE IN

INT. LIVING ROOM – DAY

DAD reading the Sunday newspapers hears an inbox mobile text tone. He reaches for his mobile on the coffee table. Reading text

TEXT
Dad – I need to talk to you – love you – xxx

DAD
(Shouting)

Come and talk to me then!

INT. BEDROOM-DAY

CAROLYN on her bed holding phone.

CAROLYN
(Shouting)

No. You come here!

INT. LIVING ROOM – DAY

DAD
(Shouting)

No!

He gets up and creeps silently out of the living room door.

INT. BEDROOM-DAY

DAD bursts in the bedroom door.

DAD
(Shouting)

What do you want?!

CAROLYN jumps out of her skin. Dad laughs and sits on the bed.

CAROLYN
Dad this is serious. I need a holiday.

DAD
You need a holiday? You drop out of college with two months to go to complete your course. You've just had your 18th birthday. You don't have a job. You have one month to go to take your GCSE Maths again so that you can improve your grade.

Are you going to tell me you are going to be revising on this holiday?

CAROLYN

Yes. I promise. The girls are booking to go to Crete. It's only £200.

DAD

Only £200? Do you know how much £200 is? No of course you don't. You've never had a job. No, No, No, No, No. It's not going to happen. You're staying here. You'll revise every day. You'll give yourself the best chance to get a a worthwhile Maths grade.

CAROLYN

I'm going.

DAD

You're not. I've got your passport.

CAROLYN
(In tears)

You don't understand. I'm deeply depressed. If I stay here I'm going to kill myself. I don't want to be here anymore. I want to die. I want to be dead and with Mum.

DAD
(angry)

Well – you've got free will now you're 18. If that's your choice. Go back to cutting yourself. You cannot go through the rest of your life making threats to get your own way. Enough is enough. Your Choice.

I love you.

He exits slamming the door.

EXT. DAD'S HOUSE – DAY

We see DAD come out of the front door distraught. He gets into his car and drives off speedily.

INT. BEDROOM-DAY

CAROLYN is equally distraught in tears – thrashing around in anger. She takes a razor out of its packet, slits her wrist.

CAROLYN
(Shattering SCREAM)

INT. CAR – DAY

DAD has pulled over and sits in his car.He HEARS the SCREAM and he gets a FLASH BACK to CAROLYN imagining her as she is. He looks worried.

He takes a passport out of his pocket. We see it is Carolyn's as he flicks through it. He hides it at the back of the glove compartment.

EXT. CAR – DAY

DAD driving off.

EXT. DAD'S HOUSE – DAY

CAROLYN stands at the front door looking normal, made up and dressed to go out handbag in hand – waiting.

DAD drives up. Unwinds the car window looking relieved to see CAROLYN smiling.

CAROLYN
Can you take me to Jane's?

Getting in the car.

INT. CAR – DAY

DAD
Jane's ?

CAROLYN
Yes. You remember Jane. I haven't seen her since
our Prom.

EXT. CAR DRIVING – DAY

> CAROLYN
>
> She's only a couple of miles away. We used to be really good friends.

INT. CAR – DAY

> CAROLYN
>
> Just want to catch up. I'll only be a couple of hours. Then if you could pick me up Daddyo – then I'll do some revision.

EXT. JANE'S PARENTS HOUSE – DAY

DAD's car pulls up, CAROLYN gets out.

> DAD
>
> A couple of hours. See you then.

INT. CAR – DAY

DAD driving happily with radio on EXT.DAD'S HOUSE – DAY

DAD pulls up in car. Gets out walks to the front door. Starts to open it. We see he is having to force it open. Something heavy is in the way. As it reaches about a foot open we see blood on the floor. He squeezes in...

INT. FRONT DOOR – DAY

We see DAD entering looking to the floor where we see CAROLYN dead.

> FADE OUT

Night Noise

Genre: Comic Suspense

Casting: 2 – Male/Female

Filming & Acting Challenge:

Sex sells! The success of this piece will depend greatly on the casting. The Woman and Man need to have chemistry.

The Woman is a highly intelligent femme fetale.

Directing this piece requires subtle lighting and a skill in building fear in the audience before any conversation begins and the burglar is revealed.

POV and reaction shots of the Woman seeing the photo and putting two and two together about the Man need to be worked out, taking the viewing audience with her revelation at the same time.

FADE IN

INT. BEDROOM – NIGHT

MAN wakes with a start. Listens frozen. Gets out of bed in pants. Stands by bedroom door quietly opens it. Listens frozen. We hear someone RUSTLING downstairs. Man quickly, quietly grabs trousers off floor puts them on hurriedly. Grabs shirt. Picks up dumb bell. Moves stealthily through door.

INT. DOWNSTAIRS LOUNGE – NIGHT

We see a hooded FIGURE all in black with a holdall filling it with valuables. Suddenly the figure stops. Listens frozen. It's nothing. Relaxes. Carries on rifling room.

Picks up laptop.

MAN

I wouldn't touch that if I was you.

FIGURE freezes. Man turns light on. FIGURE turns slowly around putting laptop down. The FIGURE is that of a WOMAN in a black catsuit with a black balaclava covering her head.

MAN

The game's up

The WOMAN seductively takes off the balaclava revealing a mischievous confident feisty pretty face.

The MAN looks pleasantly surprised

WOMAN
(indicating dumb bell. winsomely)

You won't need that.

MAN

You may be a black belt.

WOMAN
(Flirting)

More Pilates.

MAN
(angry)

What the hell are you doing in my house!

Chucking dumb bell down.

WOMAN
(Cheekily)

Being caught?

MAN
(Indicating bag)

That's my stuff!

WOMAN
(Cheekily)

I'm sorry. Is there anything that's not yours?

MAN

It's my house!

WOMAN

Sorry.

MAN

Sorry? Sorry? It's 2 o'clock in the morning! Who
are you?

WOMAN

(Flirting. Facetiously. Joking)

A spy???

As she says that her eye catches a picture of a wedding photo of a YOUNG
MARRIED COUPLE in a picture frame. The MAN freezes as she observes the
picture. We see a POV of the picture and her looking at the MAN comparing

(Nodding sagely...yes...)

A spy...I wondered why the pane of glass in the back
door was already broken. I Didn't expect anybody
to be in.

(Accusingly)

You don't read newspapers or letters stuffed through
the porch glass door – do you?

MAN

Oh – I see – you thought I was away on holiday?

WOMAN
(Flirting confidently)

I don't break panes of glass. I usually cut...

MAN

Professional.

WOMAN
(Indicating that he is an...)

Amateur.

She picks up the picture.

Not much of a likeness.

MAN
(Flirting. The game's up)

You're better looking...

WOMAN

You too...

Pause

When do you think they'll be back?

MAN

Framed – Late Honeymooners – another couple of days.

Pause

I could do with a bit of company?

Long Pause

WOMAN
(Seductively)

Mmmm. You had me worried. I thought that was also a gun in your pocket.

Walking towards him

But you're just pleased I'm here.

She kisses him

Sexy squatter...

MAN

Sexy spy....

Ravishing each other.

FADE OUT

Lonely Hearts

Genre: Suspense Drama

Casting: 6 – Leading Characters 1 Male 1 Female – 2 Police Officers 1 Male 1 Female – 2 Phone Operators 1 Male 1 Female.

Filming Challenge: This is a first date drama. The couple have communicated online. ALICE has been confident enough to invite JEREMY for a first meeting at her house for dinner.

It is important that we believe that they could genuinely make a couple; sexual chemistry between the two actors cast is essential. JEREMY needs to be charming and non-threatening.

At no time do we see how the lead up to the denouement is achieved. That needs to be left to the audience to resolve, thus adding to the shock element in the reveal.

FADE IN

EXT. HOUSE – EVENING

We see JEREMY walk to the front door. He is carrying a bottle of Red Wine and a lettuce. As he rings the bell a DOMESTIC FIRE ALARM goes off simultaneously from inside.

The door opens revealing ALICE holding a tea cloth and cooking spatula.

ALICE
(flustered)

Jeremy?

JEREMY

Yes.

ALICE

It's the steak – smoking...

JEREMY

I'll sort it. Give me the cloth – where's the alarm?

INT. ALICE'S HOUSE KITCHEN DINER – NIGHT

ALICE points towards it. JEREMY rushes to waft the cloth below it. ALICE goes to the cooker. JEREMY goes to the door and uses it as a fan to waft the smoke out and fresh air in.

The ALARM STOPS. JEREMY shuts the door – stands looking at Alice. ALICE stands looking at him from the cooker. Exhausted PAUSE.

                         ALICE
          Welcome.

They both LAUGH flirtatiously.

                         JEREMY
          I think you were hoping for a Fireman.

                         ALICE
                   (mock disappointment)
          Oh, You mean to say you're not?

                         JEREMY
          Sorry – perhaps I got the wrong house.

                         ALICE
          No – unusually you do look quite similar to your
          picture. Do you like steak?

                         JEREMY
          Well, as you've gone to such trouble to burn it –
          I mean cook it – yes.

                         ALICE
          Then you can stay.

JEREMY Going towards Alice.

                         JEREMY
          I got this for your Tortoise.

Handing her the lettuce.

ALICE
(with a flirtatious good humoured dig)

Oh you shouldn't have. She'd have been just as
happy with flowers

JEREMY
Would she also like this Red Wine?

ALICE
No, the lettuce is quite enough excitement for her
for one evening. We'll keep that for us. Here's the
corkscrew and there are the glasses.

ALICE points to the set dinner table. JEREMY goes to the table and opens and
pours wine. ALICE continues preparing final touches to food.

JEREMY holding 2 full glasses of wine walking towards Alice...

JEREMY
(mock seductively to Alice)

You're proper 'Peng'

ALICE
What?

Taking glass of wine.

JEREMY
Down with the kids – 'Peng' means 'Sexy'.

ALICE
Is **that** what you saw in my picture?

JEREMY

How could anyone resist?

They clink glasses and drink.

Embarrassed PAUSE between them both.

ALICE
Ready to eat?

JEREMY
(inferring could mean eat her)

Oh yeah!

JEREMY goes to the dinner table standing behind chairs.

Where do you want me to sit?

ALICE
There's good.

ALICE brings two plates of food to the table.

They both sit and start to eat.

PAUSE

ALICE
I'm still to find out why someone as 'Peng' – is it? – as you is single?

JEREMY
If you were to make a movie of my life – it whould be a 'U' certificate. Too nice, not mean enough.

ALICE
If only. Do you really think we women want someone mean and nasty?

JEREMY
You tell me.

ALICE
I think I want someone like you. Not 'X' rated...

JEREMY
Now – that's a result

They both laugh and clink glasses again and drink.

JEREMY
What about you? Why are you sitting there all alone?

ALICE

Not alone – I do have a tortoise. Commitment. Your gender never want to commit. I want a family – now when I have written that during the short time we have been linking up on 'Lonely Hearts' you have not unfriended me.

Now that got you a lot of brownie points. That's why I finally gave in to your outrageous 'U' rated seduction that's why Mr Too Nice you are sitting opposite me...

ALICE suddenly feels slightly dizzy and sick.

Oh dear – something's not agreed with me – I feel a bit queasy – I'm so sorry – are you all right? I hope I havn't poisoned us both.

JEREMY goes to her and stands behind her to comfort her.

JEREMY

No I'm fine. Do you want to rest on the couch?

ALICE

Yes good idea.

JEREMY walks her to the couch.

ALICE

You finish your meal.

JEREMY walks back and sits at the table eating

PAUSE

JEREMY

With cooking like this, you'll make a great wife and mum.

ALICE
(laughing)

Is that a proposal? Oh please – before I die!

Oh dear – I really think I'm feeling worse. Would you be very offended Jeremy if we called it a night.

And if you're not too put off – see each other again -
for my part I'd like to.

JEREMY
(the following two sentences should be delivered
with creepy intent, worrying the audience)

Me too. Let me help you upstairs.

ALICE
No I can manage – I'm so sorry- would you mind
going now? You're not just being polite are you? –
you havn't got a reaction to the meal?

JEREMY
No, it was if you'll forgive me 'alarmingly' tasty.

ALICE tries to raise an appreciative smile at the joke whilst getting up. Jeremy
goes to the door opening it

JEREMY
I'll be in touch.

JEREMY closes the front door behind him. Alice watches it close then makes her
way upstairs.

INT. ALICE'S BEDROOM – 3 AM NIGHT

Alice in bed stirs. She sits up. Listens intently. Slowly gets out of bed and walks to
bedroom door. Listens intently. Something is RUSTLING downstairs. She reaches
for her mobile. She is scared. She puts a chair under the handle.

Now convinced someone is in the house she dials 999.

OPERATOR 1 (V.O)
Police – fire – ambulance?

ALICE
(whispering)

Police.

OPERATOR 2 (V.O)

Police.

ALICE

Someone is in my house.

OPERATOR 2 (V.O)

What's your name and Address?

ALICE

Alice Springer – 30 Raymont Drive – Dunham – DE7 QTW – please hurry

OPERATOR 2 (V.O)

Are you on your own in the house?

ALICE

Yes

OPERATOR 2 (V.O)

Where in the house are you?

ALICE

In my bedroom.

OPERATOR 2 (V.O)

Can you lock the door?

ALICE

Ive put a chair under the handle.

OPERATOR 2 (V.O)

A patrol is in the area and will be with you shortly. Stay calm and on the line to me. I'm Gill

ALICE listens tensely. PAUSE.

We HEAR more movement.

ALICE

Gill, Please. Please what can I do? I can hear something more clearly now.

                    OPERATOR 2 (V.O)
          You'll be safe now. They have just arrived.

EXT. ALICE'S HOUSE – NIGHT

We see two police officers in uniform trying the front door.

                    POLICE OFFICER 1
          No evidence of break in there – doors locked.
          All windows look secure and not broken.

                    POLICE OFFICER 2
          You stay here – make sure no one comes out –
          I'll check the back

EXT. REAR OF ALICE'S HOUSE – NIGHT

POLICE OFFICER 2 checking door and windows.

EXT. ALICE'S HOUSE – NIGHT

POLICE OFFICER 2 returns.

                    POLICE OFFICER 2
          Nothing – no evidence of a breakin – all doors
          locked.

INT. ALICE'S BEDROOM – 3 AM NIGHT

ALICE uncontrollably frightened. Hunched up holding Mobile and a bedroom
lamp that she has unplugged with the intention of hitting someone with it if they
enter the room.

                    OPERATOR 2 (V.O)
          The officers have searched around your property
          and can see no evidence of a breakin. Has anyone
          you know got a key?

                    ALICE
          No. No. I tell you someone is in my house. Please
          help me.

                    OPERATOR 2 (V.O)
          It couldn't be a cat ?

ALICE

I don't have a cat! I have a tortoise.

OPERATOR 2 (V.O)

Well – perhaps then ...

ALICE

No. She's hibernating! Please tell the police to break down my door. Someone is in my house.

Hello? Hello?

We see her mobile phone battery has lost its charge. Frantically we see ALICE searching for a charger – she finds one but it doesn't fit being one that belonged to an older mobile. Panic stricken she chucks the mobile onto the bed and holds tightly to the Lamp looking to see if she could possibly escape through the window.

INT. ALICE'S HOUSE STAIRS – NIGHT

We see the feet of someone climbing the stairs. EXT. ALICE'S HOUSE – NIGHT

POLICE OFFICER 1 having received information from Operator 2

POLICE OFFICER 1

To POLICE OFFICER 2

The lady wants us to break down her door and rescue her.

Walking to the Police car, Police Officer 2 following.

Gill thinks she's hearing her tortoise who may have woken up from hibanating.

INT. ALICE'S BEDROOM – 3 AM NIGHT

ALICE watches as we see someone trying to push open the wedged door.

EXT. ALICE'S HOUSE – NIGHT

Police Officer 1 taking door battering device from car.

She'll be needing a new door.

Handing it to Police Oficer 2.

POLICE OFFICER 2

We'll rescue the tortoise and arrest her for animal cruelty for having woken it up.

They both laugh, nearing the front door.

INT. ALICE'S BEDROOM – 3 AM NIGHT

ALICE and we HEAR the door being bashed down followed by SILENCE. Then frantic movement of running and a scuffle with groans but no spoken words.

Pause

ALICE is now FROZEN, tears streaming down her face

POLICE OFFICER 1 (O.S)

(calling out)

Alice I'm a Police Officer. Can you let me know where you are?

Pause

ALICE

How do I know you are?

POLICE OFFICER 1 (O.S)

You were talking to Gill before your phone went dead.

ALICE sobbing opens the door. POLICE OFFICER 1 on phone.

Thank you Gill – she's safe now. Can we have an ambulance please, over and out.

Someone was in your house. We've got them now. Now Alice I want you to walk down with me looking straight ahead and out of your front door – keep looking straight ahead.

INT. ALICE'S HOUSE KITCHEN DINER – NIGHT

We see ALICE and POLICE OFFICER 1 coming down the stairs. ALICE tries her best not to look.

Then she looks.

POV of what she sees.

Every piece of furniture from earlier has been covered in plastic decorator's sheeting. Neatly laid out in an orderly fashion on the dinner table is a Chain Saw, Hack Saw, Machete and other evil-looking knives glistening with sharp malcontent.

EXT. ALICE'S HOUSE – NIGHT

We see Alice and POLICE OFFICER 1 come from the bashed down front door.

ALICE looks at the Police car. POV of what she sees

JEREMY smiling from the Police car window. He mouths 'PENG' sadistically at her.

FADE TO BLACK

Lets Be Avenue

Genre: Suspense/Comedy

Casting: 6 – 3 Male – 1 Female – 2 extras

Filming & Acting Challenge:

Casting: the Wife needs to have a sassy sexy comic allure. Burglar 2 needs to be a comic turn with his straight man, Burglar 1. The Husband has to have a masculine believable cool about him.

Directing: this requires skill in creating atmosphere and suspense of a nighttime intrusion followed by seduction and comic conclusion. The audience must think they are a kinky couple up to the reveal of them being real Police Officers at the end.

Lighting: will be a real challenge. The suspense is carried out in the dark but of course needs to be subtly lit. The majority of the comic part takes place with lights on – give it plenty of High Key Lighting.

FADE IN

INT. LARGE BEDROOM – NIGHT

Moonlit bedroom. We see MAN in bed wide awake watching a BURGLAR with a torch and gloves on at a dresser drawer taking jewellery. MAN in pyjamas creeps out of bed and grabs standing BURGLAR

from behind. There is no struggle and no vocal exclamation from either. They are both FROZEN in a silent hold. The next conversation is held in a whisper from each.

                    MAN
          You're not resisting.

                    BURGLAR
          No

                    MAN
          Aren't you scared?

213

>   BURGLAR
> Shouldn't you be?

>   MAN
> Perhaps I am.

>   BURGLAR
> I'd like to go.

>   MAN
> I know how you are feeling. Used to do what you're
> doing. Caught like you now Karma – what goes
> around comes around.

Pause.

> I'm not going to hand you in – as long as we get on
> as we are now.

>   BURGLAR
> You can let go.

MAN slowly releases his hold. BURGLAR turns to face him.

> Thanks

BURGAR'S mobile phone RINGS.

>   MAN
> I wouldn't have left that on if I was you.

BURGLAR passes it to the MAN. MAN presses ON. Listens.

> He's on his way.

Presses OFF. Hands back phone to BURGLAR. Pause.

MAN goes to door that is ajar. Starts to open it fully to gesticulate BURGLAR out.

BURGLAR 2 Bursts in with coat over his pointing arm hiding a gun. Pratt falls over dressing table stool to the ground.

WIFE in bed wakes up SCREAMING long and loud sitting up in bed in sexy bra and pants, protecting herself. She turns lightswitch on by bed. Simultaneously

BURGLAR 2 has recovered himself standing up pointing his arm covered by his coat pointing frantically at whoever looks scared enough. All others FREEZE at this.

Pause.

Then...

HUSBAND
(To wife)

Don't worry. I've got this under control.

Both BURGLARS look at each other questioningly. MAN walks over to BURGLAR 2 and triumphantly takes the coat off BURGLAR 2's arm. BURGLAR 2 is deflated as no gun is in evidence. He shakes his cramp-filled arm both hands gloved.

I think it's time you both went.

WIFE
(More relaxed)

No.

All look at her disbelievingly.

We're insured.

She gets out of bed. Takes a bag from the wardrobe. Starts to fill it with...

Designer clothes. Expensive – but once worn – well ...

You obviously need these valuables more than us.

She winks at HUSBAND and says.

Go and get them a beer darling.
You could do with a beer couldn't you?

HUSBAND exits.

BURGLARS watch her bemused and seduced by her sexy attire and now flirtatious manner.

Spect you've got little ones that need feeding Eh?

They mutter in agreement watching as she goes to her jewellery drawer and says.

Oh – you musn't miss these. £50,000 worth at least.

Holding up jewellery then putting in bag.

(Teasingly)

Oh you saw something else shiny there didn't you?

Perhaps less silvery shiny more grey.

Taking a set of handcuffs out of half open drawer.

50 shades (she giggles). These are real. Let me show
you.

Seducing them more.

You can have them. I've got two pairs. Here's the
other. A pair each. Let me put them on you. He...

(indicating HUSBAND) prefers to watch

- and I can't believe I'm saying this
- but you being here right now – you're both such
a turn on.

BURGLARS have allowed her to handcuff their hands to each other with one set
of handcuffs.

MAN (Husband) appears at door in Policeman uniform with Police Radio.

BURGLAR
(Panicking)

No Beer? Yes well. Thank you but.
We'll be definitely going now.

BURGLAR 2
Too right – not really our scene. Being watched.
Can you give us the key please?

Wife has gone to the wardrobe and taken out her Police uniform and put jacket on.

BURGLAR
Oh no! You really are into this thing. It's not for us
though...

Pause.

HUSBAND
(Enjoying their discomfort)

Not quite what you're thinking.
Turn the light out darling.

BURGLARS
(Together)

No!!

WIFE turns light out. Through the window BLUE FLASHING police light permeates the bedroom walls.

Wrong house, wrong road I'm afraid. You're in
'Let's Be Avenue'!

BURGLARS run for it.

INT. HALLWAY – NIGHT

We see them being apprehended by two officers. Marched out to car.

INT. BEDROOM – NIGHT

POLICE RADIO

13. Sergeant Wallace.

WIFE takes police radio from HUSBAND, exchanging it for pair of handcuffs she still holds.

On their way to a cell. We'll get a statement from
you tomorrow when you're both next in.

WIFE
(Into Police Radio)

13. Thank you Jim – over and out.

HUSBAND with handcuffs to WIFE

217

HUSBAND

I think I'm going to have to arrest you for being a little too seductively brave and clever!

Handcuffing her.

FADE OUT

The Goddess of Death

Genre: Sci-Fi/Comedy – for children

This is a treatment for a large cast of JUNIOR and SENIOR school young performers. Much can be improvised around the integral plot dialogue, that is written here, giving all taking part an opportunity to shine.

Characters:

SENIOR GIRLS & BOYS 14 + yr. olds

Adults: HEADMASTER – FARMER

JUNIOR GIRLS & BOYS: 9 yr. olds – 13 yr. Olds

SMALL GROUP OF TEENS: STUDENT REPORTER (son of the FARMER). JAMES. SEAN.

GODDESS OF DEATH (needs a young late-teen comedy actress)

1 – EXT. SCHOOL – NIGHT

In the dead of night through a majestic scotch pine's haunting branches we see a banner reading **Performing Arts Summer School** hanging across the front of a large Georgian building. We pan around to see a group of SENIOR BOYS (aged 15 plus) stealthily arriving below a large second floor window. Together they recite

> Oh, they do teach the torches to burn bright! It seems they hang upon the cheeks of night as rich jewels in Ethiop's ears, Beauty too rich for use, for earth too dear.

The window goes up and a liquid hit them in the face. They touch their cheeks – taste it – 'wine!'. Tied sheets are thrown out of the window. They climb up.

2 – INT/EXT. SENIOR GIRLS DORMITORY – NIGHT

Over shoulder view into the room of all the SENIOR GIRLS (aged 15 plus)in their dormitory. Giggling and flirtatious – a bottle of wine and plastic cups in evidence of chilling out.

3 – INT. SENIOR GIRLS DORMITORY – NIGHT

The last boy in and one of the girls says, 'We were expecting Romeos – but it looks like we've got Cyrano's.' One of the SENIOR BOYS hams it up with 'My nose precedes me by 15 minutes'. Laughter all round.

The next lines split amongst the SENIOR BOYS ALL SENIOR BOYS: My nose is Gargantuan!

1) You little Pig-snout, you tiny Monkey-Nostrils, you virtually invisible Pekinese-Puss,

2) Don't you realize that a nose like mine is both sceptre and orb, a monument to my superiority?

3) A great nose is the banner of a great man, a generous heart, a towering spirit, an expansive soul –

4) Such as I unmistakably am, and such as you dare not to dream of being, with your bilious weasel's eyes and no nose to keep them apart!

5) With your face as lacking in all distinction – as lacking, I say, in interest, as lacking in pride, in imagination, in honesty, in lyricism –

ALL SENIOR BOYS: in a word, as lacking in nose as that other offensively bland expanse at the opposite end of your cringing spine – which I now remove from my sight by stringent application of my boot!" they all go to kick their derrières.

SENIOR GIRLS 'OK – OK – thank you – we'll let you know – next – they are hams that cannot be cured'.

SENIOR GIRLS 'Ok boys your turn'. SENIOR BOYS 'but first – where did you get the wine'. SENIOR GIRLS 'OK – that's our truth question'. SENIOR BOYS 'No, No no no!'. SENIOR GIRLS 'Yes, yes, yes, yes – Sophie's dad is a wine merchant.'

SOPHIE 'Yea and I help him and myself on Saturdays – nuff said'. SENIOR GIRLS 'Truth or Dare'. SENIOR BOYS 'we've just done our dare – and that wasn't our question. So, girls' truth or dare?' SENIOR GIRLS 'Oh all right – Truth'. SENIOR BOYS 'O.K. Your Romeo has been magically transformed into an animal, and the only way to restore your love is to mate with them. Here's the question: Which animal would cause you the least psychological damage?'. (Girls devise answers). SENIOR GIRLS 'Boys Truth or Dare'. SENIOR BOYS 'Dare'. The girls huddle together to discuss. SENIOR GIRLS 'OK – here goes – You remember our conversation earlier about crop circles – we dare you to prove your point and go out into the corn fields and make some as you said you could.' SENIOR BOYS huddle together to discuss. SENIOR BOYS 'OK – but only if we can make it a party. That is, we all go ...and ... and the next truth or dare from you lot has to be a DARE.'. SENIOR GIRLS 'Deal – let's use some of the torches we've got for the open-air production of *A Midsummer Night's Dream* – boys wake and bring the other geeks from your dormitory – we can then perform *A Midsummer Night's Dream*. SENIOR BOYS 'Will do – but we must not wake the juniors – we don't want them coming along to spoil the fun'. SENIOR GIRLS 'We'll meet you by the front entrance'.

4 – INT. JUNIORS GIRLS DORMITORY – NIGHT

The Juniors are up – the JUNIOR BOYS visiting the girls – a group are at a Ouija Board. Finishing the letters of CELLAR and another group playing Botticelli.

The Botticelli Group – making a bit of noise 'we've got to be quieter – we don't want to wake the SENIORS'.

1) The Dark Knight – were you the Joker in a film by that name behaving slightly Batty 2) Yes, I am Heath Ledger 1) My Turn – My turn! –

The Ouija Board Group.

A) I live in the Cellar B) Oh my God C) (to the Botticelli group) we've got a girl who's dead and lives here in the cellar D) Ask how she died

One of them leaves the board, backing off scared – there is a pause of spooked fear

Botticelli Group

3) We told you you shouldn't do that stuff'

4) (a Joker pretending to empathise with them – telling tale very seriously) When I was younger, about seven, I was playing, and I saw the cellar door open – just a crack. Now my Mum and Dad had always warned me – (name) whatever you do don't go near the cellar door. So of course, I had to see what was on the other side if it killed me. So, I went to the cellar door, pushed it and walked through, and I saw strange, wonderful things – things I had never seen before – like ...trees, grass, flowers, the sun

– The others chuck pillows at him – making a noise.

One of the GIRLS quietens them down. 'Shush...I hear something'. Someone else 'It's the girl from the cellar!'. They are quiet.

5 – INT. UPSTAIRS CORRIDOR.

NIGHT

SENIOR BOYS creeping past on their way out.

6 – INT. JUNIORS GIRLS DORMITORY.

NIGHT

Whisper 'I'm scared'. There is a tap at the window. All look towards it. The lights go out. We see silhouetted a dark shape coming from behind the curtain – slowly moving into the room. The lights switch back on. It is someone in a scream mask with blood streaming from it –a bundle ensues – and the culprit is unmasked giggling away – their accomplice, the joker, at the lights. A)'Told you not to play with that Ouija board stuff'   B)'You gave it to us' – A) & Joker 'stitch up – stitch – up!'

7 – EXT. PROPS SHED – NIGHT

SENIOR GIRLS getting torches

8 – EXT.WOODSHED. NIGHT Discussing how to make the circles – SENIOR BOYS getting 2 x 2 wood and string etc

9 – EXT.OUTSIDE SCHOOL – NIGHT

Owls and other nocturnal creatures permeate the night stillness with their familiar haunting sounds. A loud screech – cut to a snarling Close Up of a startled cat frightening the girls and audience alike. SENIOR GIRLS light the torches.

10 – EXT.FRONT OF SCHOOL.NIGHT

SENIOR GIRLS and SENIOR BOYS group together around JOSH & CLAIRE. 'Come on this way'

11 – INT. JUNIOR GIRL'S DORMITORY – NIGHT

JUNIOR GIRLS sending JUNIOR BOYS back to their room. 'We're going to sleep now'. JUNIOR BOY A 'I'll take my board back tomorrow – just leave it well alone till then. By the way I know how she died – it was about 1908– a family moved in here with a little girl called Martha. She and her brother were playing hide and seek – but she never could be found. Tomorrow if you look in the cellar you'll find what they used to call a priest's hole from when they used to hide Catholic priests in Elizabeth 1st's reign. She found it, her family never did. Trouble is once in she could never get out'. Gob smacked silence. JUNIOR GIRL 'How do you know that?' JUNIOR BOY mysteriously taps his nose and exits leaving the JUNIOR GIRLS awe-struck.

12 – EXT. PATHWAY TO FIELD – NIGHT

SENIOR BOYS & GIRLS walking with their victuals of wine and crisps, fags etc towards a cornfield. With them they carry the two by two pieces of wood 'This will be over all the newspapers tomorrow 'CROP CIRCLES IN BEDFORDSHIRE – VISITORS FROM THE PLANET ZOG – they all laugh excitedly continuing on their way climbing over a fence. SALLY 'Well I don't think they are made like the boys are going to to make them – I think they are real' GEORGE 'Yeah – as real as Harry Potter' JOSH 'Just you wait and see Sally – ours will look like all the rest – and so what will that tell you'?

13 – EXT.CORNFIELD NIGHT

SENIOR GIRLS 'Now boys get to work for your dare – geometric shapes measuring the radius with cuts of string like you said'. They start to create the shapes.

14 – INT. SCHOOL HEAD'S BEDROOM – NIGHT HEADMASTER fast asleep.

15 – INT. JUNIOR BOYS DORMITORY – NIGHT JUNIOR BOYS Asleep

16 – INT. JUNIOR GIRLS DORMITORY – NIGHT

We pan across from the Ouija Board still laid out to see the JUNIOR GIRLS asleep

17 & 18 – EXT. CORNFIELD – NIGHT CROSS CUTTING between following scene and SENIOR BOYS making crop circle.

TITANIA's Lines shared by all the girls as a Chorus while walking around ritualistically.

> ... The ploughman lost his sweat,
>
> and the green corn Hath rotted ere his youth attain'd a beard; The fold stands empty in the drowned field, And crows are fatted with the murrion flock; The nine men's morris is fill'd up with mud, And the quaint mazes in the wanton green For lack of tread are undistinguishable: The human mortals want their winter here; No night is now with hymn or carol blest: Therefore the moon, the governess of floods, Pale in her anger, washes all the air, That rheumatic diseases do abound: And thorough this

distemperature we see The seasons alter: hoary-headed frosts Far in the fresh lap of the crimson rose, And on old Hiems' thin and icy crown An odorous chaplet of sweet summer buds Is, as in mockery, set: the spring, the summer, The childing autumn, angry winter, change Their wonted liveries, and the mazed world, By their increase, now knows not which is which: And this same progeny of evils comes From our debate, from our dissension; We are their parents and original.

HERMIA God speed fair Helena! wither away?

ELENA Call you me fair? that fair again unsay. Demetrius loves your fair: O happy fair!

HERMIA I frown upon him, yet he loves me still.

HELENA O that your frowns would teach my miles such skill!

HERMIA I give him curses, yet he gives me love.

HELENA O that my prayers could such affection move!

HERMIA The more I hate, the more he follows me.

HELENA The more I love, the more he hateth me.

HERMIA His folly, Helena, is no fault of mine.

HELENA None, but your beauty: would that fault were mine!

HERMIA Take comfort: he no more shall see my face; Lysander and myself will fly this place.

SENIOR BOY Nerd: Helena's problem is Cyrano's – unrequited love

SENIOR BOYS 'Yeah yeah yeah yeah – Enough no more – tis not so sweet now as it was before – How sweet the moonlight sleeps upon this bank – here will we sit and let the sounds of music creep in our ears – soft stillness and the night become the touches of sweet harmony'. SENIOR GIRLS start to sing a contemporaneous pop song.

SENIOR BOYS 'We'll just have a bit more to drink girls and then it'll be time for your dare.' One starts to say as he passes the bottle around "Another little drink wouldn't do us any harm Pierces through the sabbatical calm. And that is the place for me!"

The rest of the boys follow, quoting more from Edith Sitwell's *Facade* as they continue to chill with the SENIOR GIRLS still singing and dancing:

So, do not take a bath in Jordan, Gordon, On the holy Sabbath on the peaceful day – Or you'll never go to heaven, Gordon Macpherson, and speaking purely as a private person that is the place – that is the place – that is the place for me!

A rowdy crescendo with all partying.

19 – EXT. A FARMHOUSE – NIGHT

Shot of a distant farm house with music coming from it. In through the window a party is coming to its end with the few remaining stragglers – we meet all the characters who will be THE SENIOR REPORTERS the following morning. One needs to mention 'a younger sister or younger brother being out of the way at the Acting School nearby'. (Devise party scene)

20 – EXT.CORNFIELD – NIGHT

They have mostly merrily collapsed in the full moonlight – joking and fooling about. SENIOR GIRLS 'Time to get the next one done boys – put all you litter in this bag – anything left will lead people to think it's a prank.'

SENIOR BOYS 'But first – your dare'. GIRLS 'OK – what is it to be?'. BOYS 'All of you stand in a circle – right we are going to spin this bottle – whichever one of you it points at has 30 seconds to hide in the field. The others can cover our eyes. We then have 30 seconds to find you. If we do ALL of you have to take all your clothes off and hold a pose for 5 seconds. Devised dialogue much protestation GIRLS 'We'll get you for this' – agreement – bottle spins – points at one of them – they start to run after the other girls cover the BOYS eyes.

Suddenly a tremendous force like a tornado accompanied by an unearthly sound blows them all to the ground. We see close up shots of them trying to resist and bright lights flashing onto their faces as they are looking up to the sky frightened and awe-struck by what they are seeing. We do not see IT only experiencing IT from their terror of what we imagine the cause to be. Silence – then tears – relief IT has gone. 'CLAIRE & JOSH 'Look – we didn't make those' SALLY 'I told you they were real – we shouldn't have been messing with what we don't understand'. We see elaborate crop circles that could not have been created by them. Then in the middle of one a bright light ignites then fades leaving a glistening pulsating

ORB the size of a football. As one they all walk towards it, hypnotised, saying nothing – we see the look on their faces in individual close ups – they surround it and all stare. In unison they all laugh as if it has told them a hysterical joke – the ORB starts to levitate - no words are spoken.

21 – EXT. PATHWAY BACK TO SCHOOL – NIGHT

WE see SENIOR BOYS & GIRLS being led towards the school following as one in silence as if being instructed by the ORB – all are under its spell.

22 – EXT. CORNFIELD – NIGHT

We cut to see in the middle of the crop circle they created - their rubbish blowing across into the other circles not made by them and their wood and string scattered and left with bottles of wine.

23 – INT. SENIOR GIRLS DORMITORY – NIGHT

Cut to seeing from inside the room the last SENIOR in. The door shuts automatically. Cut to the ORB placed in the middle of the room controlling them. The outer case shatters to reveal a CRYSTAL SKULL. There is a reaction and one of the SENIOR GIRLS screams, snapping them out of their hypnotic state.

24 – INT. SCHOOL HEADS BEDROOM - NIGHT

Cut to the HEADMASTER being woken.

25 – INT. SENIOR GIRLS DORMITORY - NIGHT

Cut back to the SENIORS having been snapped out of their hypnotic state. Fear and excitement are shared in their conversation.

26 – INT. UPSTAIRS CORRIDOR - NIGHT

Cut to the HEADMASTER walking to find out what is happening.

27 – INT. SENIOR GIRLS DORMITORY - NIGHT

The door opens. HEADMASTER 'Now – come on what are you all up to? Its 2 o'clock in the morning – and I definitely think you should all now be trying to get some sleep for the rehearsal **this morning!** (seeing the skull) very impressive – and where did you get that - is it a prop from the Indiana Jones movie *Kingdom of the Crystal Skull*?'. HEADMASTER walking towards it. The children move back in fear trying to warn him. The HEADMASTER shushes them and seemingly now hypnotised touches it. Instantly his Doppelganger appears. We are in the presence of TWO IDENTICAL HEADMASTERS. All react again. The HEADMASTER

DOPPLEGANGER 'At last we are to be released – You (indicating some SENIORS) tie him up with that sheet. (covering his ears) Oh what a strange sound you people make. (Staccato robotic delivery) At – the – moment – I – don't – know quite – what – I – think – until – I – hear – myself – say – it. Oh yes, I meant that. What a funny Language – language? – language? – Oh yes is that what **you** call it? – yes **Language**. It's too exhausting – I'll speak to you again for now, through your minds!' The SENIORS once again appear hypnotised and do as they are told. We hear the HEADMASTER (Telepathically) say 'Now this won't take long – each take turns to touch TRISKAIDEKA'. Each SENIOR touches the TRISKAIDEKA SKULL and instantly their DOPPLEGANGER appears. They are now in lines facing themselves. One of the SENIOR GIRLS says, 'do I really look like that?' Her DOPPLEGANGER replies 'I'm afraid so – painful isn't it'. All the DOPPELGANGERS laugh. The SENIOR GIRL gives a wide-eyed vacant cheek attitude 'Ugh?'. The DOPPLEGAGERS speak the following words robotically, individually one after the other. 'You – are – now – under – our – control – and – for – now – will – not – be – able – to – leave – this – room – it – is – a shielded – vacuum – from – which – you – cannot – leave'. The HEADMASTER DOPPELGANGER picks up the TRISKAIDEKA SKULL saying out loud 'CHARRIONS – follow me'. All the SENIOR DOPPELGANGERS follow out of the room.

28 – INT.STAIRCASE – NIGHT

Cut to seeing the SENIOR DOPPELGANGERS walking down the staircase to the HEADMASTER'S study.

29 – INT/EXT. HEADMASTERS STUDY – NIGHT

SENIOR DOPPELGANGERS Walking into the study.

30 – INT. HEADMASTERS STUDY – NIGHT

We see the SKULL being placed in a prominent position by the HEADMASTER. All the SENIOR DOPPELGANGERS watch. HEADMASTER 'CHARRIONS We now are here – and you will soon have all the power you need for your journey'. SENIORS DOPPELGANGERS gesticulating in a robotic manner 'Yes – the – energy – we – are – getting – from – these – capsules – is – as – we – expected' they all mutter agreement 'these – young – Homo – Sapiens – will – give – us – time – to – achieve – our – goal'. As each SENIOR speaks their voices change and faces morph in Close Up to a GREY ALIEN visage and then back to their features. HEADMASTER morphing 'as your CHARRION ELDER I have had to become this older capsule, and this is an energy that will lose power – you will have to protect me from this Homo sapiens GOOD SOUL'. They all laugh in a terrifyingly knowing sinister manner.

31 – INT. SENIOR GIRLS DORMITORY – NIGHT

The SENIOR BOYS & GIRLS in the bedroom are moving and talking as if struggling through treacle – their normal personalities are present, but energy levels depleted as the DOPPLEGANGERS draw on their energy. JOSH & CLAIRE are trying to take control and organise untying the HEADMASTER who is drained and asleep. They lie him down on a bed. CLAIRE 'That was a Crystal Skull – like STEVE said when he walked in – the Indiana Jones film – *Kingdom of The Crystal Skull* – but that was no prop!' JOSH 'Yeah – I read up on them only the other day – ancient South American Maya Indian legend says there were 13 Crystal Skulls belonging to THE GODDESS OF DEATH. All appear suitably, fearfully apprehensive. 'Over the past centuries 5 of them have been discovered by archaeologists and either kept by them and their families or gifted to museums. Eight are yet to be found. CLAIRE 'Seven'. All acknowledge what she is inferring. JOSH 'Yes – now with this one only seven – you're right – if this **is** – the thing is they say that if all are brought together again life as we know it will never be the same again'. ClAIRE 'And don't we know it!'. All are now seriously frightened. SALLY 'But that does not mean it has to be for the worse – I saw a documentary about them and it said that when all thirteen are all together we will learn great things about our past and our future –the Maya legend says they will give us the answers to our existence and help us – no more wars and poverty'. CLAIRE 'Are you mad – THE GODDESS OF DEATH and look at what is happening to us now'.

32 – EXT. CORNFIELD – DAWN

A small group of SENIOR STUDENT REPORTERS presenting to camera 'The farmer who owns this land is extremely angry that his crop has been ruined in this way – who do you think is responsible?' FARMER 'Kids having a prank – must have been a lot of them mind – look – candle torches, wine bottles and cigarette butts are everywhere. If they wanted us to believe it was Aliens they should have cleaned up after them – too much to expect of this generation – they wouldn't litter their own homes like this, though would they?'. STUDENT REPORTER 'All right DAD – don't go on – cut'. FARMER 'You do mind (litter home)! This should help you lot and your Media Studies SON – you should be able to sell this to the local TV News station – I told you it was worth getting up for. Good job you lot were all staying over after your party last night.' JAMES 'Why don't we clean up all the mess – and pretend it's real – that would be good enough for National news coverage'. FARMER 'Yeah and when you get found out – as you would – the end of a promising career for you all'. Sean 'I've a better idea – I am not one of you Mickie Mouse namby pamby Media Studies students – I am going to have a real job!' GROUP 'OK Sherlock Holmes – what do you suggest?' SEAN 'Exactly – that's what I'm going to be and that's what we are going to do now – for your DAD we will detect who was responsible for this and get them to confess on camera – like they do in those TV exposure programmes. FARMER 'Now you're talking – that'll make an even better local news story for you all – students unearth hoax'. SEAN 'Yes, and I already have an idea it has something to do with that Performing Arts Summer School over there that your sister/brother is at'.

33 – INT. HEADMASTER'S STUDY – DAWN

HEADMASTER & SENIOR DOPPELGANGERS are circling the CRYSTAL SKULL in ritual, they intone 'GODDESS OF DEATH we see you'.

From the SKULL appears THE GODDESS OF DEATH transported from Planet Charrion (She is dressed and made up like an extreme modern-day GOTH)

GODDESS 'Phew – what a journey!' dusting herself off. The SENIOR DOPPELGANGERS do a choreographed stand, turn, kneel, & bow of their heads.

GODDESS 'Oh stop all that (double take) Oh – you look almost human!' all laugh morphing to their Alien personas and back.

GODDESS 'Don't spoil it! Those capsules you inhabit were made in *my* image when our creator CHAOS asked me to create my own experiment on this TERRESTRIAL ORB. (touching the globe) Out of all the ORBS in all the UNIVERSES this has always been *my* favourite of course for that reason. You have *your* own favourite ORB that carries *your* likeness – (teasing them) though personally I often think looking at the likes of you I got the better deal. I mean just look at – us!' looking at herself in the mirror – nothing is reflected back –SENIOR DOPPELGANGERS laugh.

GODDESS 'Oh – yes I forgot – in my image – but we CHARRIONS have no SOUL as these *MUTANT* HUMANOIDS call it and so are unable to see ourselves. It's enough to make you weep!

She acts a weeping episode – the SENIOR DOPPELGANGERS imitate her, sending up HUMAN emotions.

GODDESS 'But of course – we cannot weep as these MUTANTS have developed – only laugh'

They all laugh

SENIOR DOPPLEGANGERS (once again sharing the dialogue robotically) 'soon you will be able to see yourself *and* we will all be able to weep with joy – *our destiny* – you created all these humanoids and you will consume all of them – it is in *your nature* GODDESS OF DEATH (they laugh). And then we will have the secret to how they have mutated from HUMANOIDS like ourselves – to having this mutation inside themselves that they call a *SOUL* that gives them the weeping emotion. Of all the creations in all the universes we CHARRIONS need this mutation to be able to travel without our crafts as spirits to other dimensions where we will find and conquer our creator CHAOS who is saying these HUMANS are more interesting and affectionate than us. (mock CHAOS as being dumb pointing to heads) Durr...This is how we will save CHARRION and no longer will there be (said with nasty taste in mouth) *HUMAN SOULS* fluttering about all over CHARRION creating dimensional interference. They are *so boring* when they sometimes get through to try and teach us how to have *feelings*'

GODDESS 'Quite so – Quite so! But to be honest *you* are becoming quite *boring* yourselves droning on from those capsules you are inhabiting – oh dear did I hurt your HUMAN *feelings?*'.

SENIOR DOPPELGANGERS 'Ugh' they shudder at the thought of such things.
GODDESS 'But I suppose it would take me too long to teach you how to speak properly like me. And *long* is not what we have. The excitement is too great! Oh look – that over there is Inspiration Water that I saw your capsule (to HEADMASTER) enjoy while I was watching from CHARRION last night. Do what he did – put it in a glass and tip it down this hole (pointing to her mouth) for us to celebrate what is to be – our destiny – to unite TRISKAIDEKA here with all the other 12 CRYSTAL SKULLS that we scattered around this ORB when we gave it Humanoid life in my likeness. When you have succeeded in using your capsules energy to transport yourselves to find them and bring them here – so that the twelve may join TRISKAIDEKA (touching the skull) we will take them to where you beamed down – and there will be our *destiny* – as the great knowledge of these HUMANOID MUTANTS that these SKULLS have been recording in their crystals will be transported to our CENTRAL CRYSTAL on CHARRION where they will tell us how it is that these creatures mutated a *SOUL* that we did not create.'

SENIOR DOPPELGANGERS 'Then WE too will be able to see into our SOULS and love our reflections.'

There is a moment while the GODDESS does a double take at such a thought of the ugly CHARRIONS seeing & loving their reflection.

GODDESS 'Yes and then you may have cause to weep

They all in unison give her a mock hurt look

GODDESS These Mutant Humanoids superstition of the number 13 – Triskaidekaphobia – as they call it – will have been proved to be correct – The power of our 13 CRYSTAL SKULLS in unison will consume all their SOULS for me GODDESS OF DEATH – it will be my final SOULUTION!'.

They all groan at her bad joke.

GODDESS 'Um – poor me another – it's making me feel quite HUMAN'.
SENIOR DOPPELGANGERS – 'UGH'

backing away and then laughing and pouring her another drink.

34 – INT. SENIOR GIRLS DORMITORY – DAWN

SENIORS who have been listening with glasses to the floor to the conversation below. Consternation and discussion ensue 'How are we going to stop them?' etc. SENIORS 'It's just as we said and there is a Goddess of Death!'

35 – INT. JUNIOR GIRLS DORMITORY – DAWN

The girls are asleep – there is a scratching sound – one of them slowly wakes wondering what the noise is – we pan with her viewpoint to the Ouija Board – the planchette is moving on its own across the letters – she wakes the others – they all look in fear being drawn to see what the board is saying. 'ALIENS' They scream and run out.

36 – INT. HEADMASTER'S STUDY – DAWN

SENIOR DOPPELGANGERS 'What is that?'

GODDESS 'Oh it will be all those sweet little JUNIOR ones getting ready for breakfast.'

SENIOR DOPPELGANGERS 'Ugh'

They bridle at the thought of human children.

GODDESS 'Do not worry – you have work to do – while you are transporting I and the HEADMASTER here will make sure no one can get into this room'.

HEADMASTER 'It will be sealed'

GODDESS 'Meanwhile HEADMASTER I want you to introduce me to these little JUNIOR HUMANS as their new Performing Arts Teacher. I feel in the mood for a bit of fun'.

SENIOR DOPPELGANGERS 'Ugh'

Once again bridling at the thought of Human children.

37 – INT. JUNIOR BOYS DORMITORY – DAWN

JUNIOR GIRLS 'We tell you the thing – whatever i'ts called ...'

JUNIOR BOY

'Planchette'

JUNIOR GIRLS 'Was moving on its own and spelled out ALIENS!'

JUNIOR BOYS 'Yeah – very funny – we'll see you at breakfast – if we don't watch it we'll miss it – we're going to be late.

JUNIOR GIRLS 'It's true'

JUNIOR BOYS 'Go'

38 – INT. SENIOR GIRLS DORMITORY – DAWN

SENIORS 'The Goddess is getting drunk – she likes drink – but cannot take it – perhaps that's how we could I can hear the JUNIORS call out for them to come and help.

They try to get out of the door and windows and call out.

SENIOR 'Remember they said we were sealed in a vacuum – that's just what it is – we are making all this noise – we are banging and shouting – but they cannot hear us. It is as if this room has been sound-proofed – we cannot open the doors or windows – we can hear sound coming in but they obviously can hear nothing coming out. It's as if we are inside a vacuum.

JOSH – Perhaps they have put us in a worm hole – a black hole'

SENIOR 'A dumb hole'.

SENIOR 'In space no one can hear you scream'.

They all react to this.

39 – INT. BREAKFAST ROOM – DAY

JUNIOR BOYS & GIRLS are gathered helping themselves to cornflakes etc.

JUNIOR BOY 1 'You know the girls said Aliens'

JUNIOR BOY 2 'Well – I dreamt of a SKULL – it was no ordinary Skull – and it came in a spaceship.'

JUNIOR BOY 1 'You can't have – that's what I dreamt of!'

JUNIOR BOY 3 'And me'

Word spreads amongst them all – the girls slowly remember the same –

JUNIOR GIRLS (realising significance) Aliens

All have had a similar dream. Suddenly beside them appears THE GODDESS OF DEATH from nowhere

GODDESS 'Well – I wonder what could have caused that then'.

All scream

GODDESS 'Oh Headmaster please – come in and explain'.

HEADMASTER (comes into the room) 'Don't worry – THEA DOGFODDESS is a surprise guest teacher that I have specially arranged for you today'. (As he says this his face morphs into his Alien persona and back.)

GODDESS (whispering) 'Go back – you must lie down – you're in an old capsule and losing power'.

JUNIORS (whispering) 'Did you see what happened to STEVE then?'. **HEADMASTER** 'Don't worry – you are in safe...(notices hands are changing – hides behind his back)'

GODDESS (to him) 'Go go go'.

She shuffles him out of the French doors as he struggles with his transformation back to a CHARRION ALIEN.

GODDESS 'Yes what STEVE did not tell you – is that I am a special guest specialising in – magic! – First lesson – now what you are eating all looks rather dreary – wouldn't you prefer to have this...

The corn flakes etc are changed to McDonald type burgers – (no packaging avoid advertising specific chain) gasp in disbelief as they react some screaming, some screaming with delight.

40 – EXT. SCHOOL DRIVE – DAY

News Reporter Students coming down the drive – 'listen to that – Drama Students over acting as usual'.

41 – EXT. SENIOR GIRLS DORMITORY WINDOW – DAY Seniors looking out of the window at them trying to attract their attention.

42 – INT. SENIOR GIRLS DORMITORY WINDOW – DAY POV of Reporters coming down the drive

43 – INT. BREAKFAST ROOM – DAY

GODDESS 'Now second lesson'.

THEA DOGFODDESS appears again from another position.

JUNIOR 4 (sarcastically) 'Do you have to keep on doing that – why not walk like everyone else'

The GODDESS spikes her hand at the JUNIOR 4's burger – it instantly changes to a large juicy slug.

GODDESS 'Anyone else have any complaints?' Silence 'Now as I was saying – the second lesson I want to teach you is...'

44 – INT. SENIOR GIRLS DORMITORY – DAY

POV of HEADMASTER DOPPELGANGER through window in garden.

SENIORS 'Look at what 's happened to Steve Down There'

We see his HEADMASTER DOPPELGANGER has fully morphed back into the ELDER CHARRION ALIEN

STEVE's energy having been released has been waking up during this time and is now standing.

HEADMASTER STEVE 'what's happening?' All turn to see him

SENIORS 'Look Steve – look you were down there'.

He looks through the window and sees himself with morphed head and hands.

CLAIRE ' I get it – they created a clone from us and are keeping us running like batteries somehow drawing on our energy – Steve has woken up and his supply of energy to his clone has weakened the clone's resistance and the alien inside is manifesting itself.'

JOSH 'The stronger we all get the more likely it is that our clones will no longer hide the parasite alien inside'.

SENIOR 'The CHARRION – they called themselves CHARRIONS.'

HEADMASTER STEVE 'Come on – all follow me'

SENIORS 'We can't – they have trapped us in this room.'

45 – EXT. SCHOOL – DAY

We see SENIOR REPORTERS spot ELDER CHARRION ALIEN

HEADMASTER they hide and watch

SENIOR REPORTERS 'Whey ...look at that ...etc'

Then suddenly **he vanishes** – SENIOR REPORTERS look at each other in disbelief.

46 – INT. BREAKFAST ROOM – DAY

We see all the JUNIORS huddled around a PLASMA SCREEN the ELDER CHARRION ALIEN HEADMASTER **Beams in** standing next to the TV to switch it on.

GODDESS 'Now if you are all ready – here your second lesson comes – watch the screen'.

ELDER CHARRION ALIEN HEADMASTER switches it on. the following scene from the headmaster's study is playing through.

47 – INT. HEADMASTERS STUDY – DAY

We see a close up of the CRYSTAL SKULL pulling back to reveal all of the SENIOR DOPPELGANGERS – one at a time they touch the skull and instantly disappear. When all have gone we close in on the CRYSTAL SKULL – it vanishes – we cut straight to scene 49.

48 – INT. SENIOR GIRL'S DORMITORY – DAY

CROSS CUTTING with previous scene but this scene not shown on the plasma screen.

SENIORS fall to the ground into a deep sleep in exactly the position they are in as each one of their SENIOR DOPPELGANGERS vanish from the PLASMA SCREEN screen.

HEADMASTER STEVE is left standing, surrounded by them all inert on the floor horrified. Out of the window we have seen flashes of **lightening** energy representing the clones flying off through the air on their mission.

49 – INT. BREAKFAST ROOM – DAY

The plasma screen instantly cuts out as the CRYSTAL SKULL disappears on screen. The JUNIORS look around to the GODDESS to see her hands out stretched towards the screen and the CRYSTAL SKULL suddenly appear in her hands.

50 – EXT. SCHOOL – DAY

SENIOR REPORTERS 'First that weird looking dood looked as if it disappeared and it had a pretty realistic mask on as well' etc. 'it was so good – I wanted to applaud when it vanished like that and what a finale with all the **lightening** – I think we should get some tickets for the show – let's ask how they did it – Come on ring the doorbell'.

51 – INT. BREAKFAST ROOM – DAY

We hear the very loud DOOR BELL. The Juniors are now petrified unable to take their eyes off ELDER CHARRION ALIEN HEADMASTER STEVE.

GODDESS (holding the Crystal Skull) 'would you all like to answer the door for us'

JUNIORS (in unison seeing this as a chance to escape) 'Yes!'.

GODDESS 'Well you cannot – this rooms is now sealed – for your own safety of course – I'll take TRISKAIDEKA here with me and leave your new HEAD (she laughs at her joke) to explain himself while I answer the door.

She goes.

52 – INT. HEADMASTER'S STUDY – DAY

GODDESS rushes in puts down SKULL – grabs the bottle of whisky – hurriedly takes a swig – exits.

53 – INT. STAIRCASE – DAY GODDESS runs up the staircase.

54 – INT.CORRIDOR – DAY

GODDESS rushing to SENIOR GIRLS DORMITORY

55 – INT. SENIOR GIRLS DORMITORY – DAY

GODDESS bursts in. HEADMASTER STEVE turns around in midst of sleeping SENIORS that he has been trying to wake up.

GODDESS 'You need to answer the door – didn't you hear the bell ring?'

HEADMASTER STEVE (confused) 'who are you?'

GODDESS 'I have come to rescue you all – but first for your own safety tell whoever it is at the door – to come back another day'

HEADMASTER STEVE 'And if I don't?'

GODDESS 'All of you will die'.

56 – EXT. SCHOOL FRONT DOOR – DAY

STUDENT REPORTERS 'Come on – let's just walk in – it's a school – why are we ringing the bell anyway – there will be a reception inside'

They enter.

57A – INT. STAIRCASE/HALLWAY – DAY

STEVE coming down the staircase followed by GODDESS – turning the corner – bump into STUDENT REPORTERS.

SEAN 'Oh – Hello –as no one had answered – we thought there must be a reception we could leave a note at'.

GODDESS 'What – to say you had robbed the safe – thank you very much!'.

SEAN 'No! we are here to ask a few questions about crop circles'.

GODDESS (laughs hysterically)

All look at her, including HEADMASTER STEVE who is more bemused than anyone.

HEADMASTER STEVE 'Crop circles?'.

57B – INT. STAIRCASE/HALLWAY – DAY

Same as above – **without** GODDESS in shot.

58 – INT. BREAKFAST ROOM – DAY

The JUNIORS are sitting watching ELDER HEADMASTER CHARRION ALIEN STEVE who has fallen asleep – they try to escape but find the same as the others had – that they are sealed in. Whispered conversation along the lines of let's tie him up – good idea – very quietly that is what they do, finding a box of skipping ropes.

GEAK (who has been writing reveals) 'we were told the GOTH Teacher's name was THEA DOGFODDESS. Its an anagram – all the letters moved around from that name spell out GODDESS OF DEATH'.

In unison all the JUNIORS try to escape, bashing at the windows and doors. ALIEN STEVE is shocked awake.

59 – EXT. BREAKFAST ROOM FRENCH WINDOWS – DAY

We see but hear nothing of the JUNIORS TRYING frantically to escape.

60 – INT/EXT.SCHOOL FRONT DOOR.

DAY STUDENT REPORTERS being shown out.

GODDESS 'Sorry we cannot help – perhaps they really were made by Aliens from outer space'

She roars with laughter, slamming the door in their faces.

61 – EXT. SCHOOL FRONT DOOR – DAY STUDENT REPORTERS

SEAN 'I don't believe a word they said – I reckon they know that their students were responsible and are trying to cover up for them'.

STUDENT REPORTER 1 'If only we had that interview on camera – we could show them up as liars.

STUDENT REPORTER 2 'We did – we were filming secretly through the bag – just like investigative programmes do'

SEAN 'Now that is ace – really – let's have a look'.

STUDENT REPORTERS 'Let's get further away from here first'.

62 – INT. HEADMASTERS STUDY – DAY

GODDESS (helping herself to more drink) 'Are you sure you won't have one while we wait my warriors return'.

HEADMASTER STEVE 'Where are the other children?'

GODDESS 'Oh – very well – follow me'

62B – INT.BREAKFAST ROOM – DAY

JUNIORS milling about still trying to escape.

63 – EXT. FRENCH WINDOWS BREAKFAST ROOM – DAY

JUNIORS see HEADMASTER STEVE outside and rush to ask his help – but once again like a bad dream he cannot hear them only see their pleading. He focuses in alarm on ELDER CHARRION HEADMASTER STEVE who has broken free from being tied up and is horrified at seeing an ALIEN close up for the first time.

64 – EXT/INT. FRENCH WINDOWS BREAKFAST ROOM. DAY

GODDESS (opening the door – then we hear their screams and pleadings) 'Oh dear – Oh dear – Why are you making such a DIN is it DIN-NER TIME'

she once again roars with laughter. HEADMASTER STEVE helpless follows in behind her – they become absolutely silent as ELDER CHARRION HEADMASTER ALIEN STEVE continues to laugh.

GODDESS (goes to ALIEN STEVE whispers in his ear)

ALIEN STEVE vanishes

GEEK 'you are the GODDESS OF DEATH – what are you going to do with us?'.

GODDESS (to STEVE) 'Oh, you have a clever one here – well what do you think I could do with you – Um?'.

Silence

65 – EXT, WOODS – DAY

STUDENT REPORTERS crouched down in the wood watching the footage. We also see a POV shot of the footage.

SEAN 'Where is she?'

STUDENT REPORTERS 'you tell us Sherlock'.

We see some more footage hearing the GODDESS'S voice in the conversation.

SEAN 'We can hear her – but not see her'.

STUDENT REPORTERS 'We never did ask how they did that vanishing trick'.

SEAN 'Yeah – well I don't fancy asking her now'.

STUDENT REPORTERS 'This wood, is spooky enough without all this – let's get back to the farm'.

As they turn, ELDER CHARRION HEADMASTER ALIEN STEVE is standing watching them – petrified they stand and watch as one after the other SENIOR CLONES appear as ALIENS holding a CRYSTAL SKULL each and staring menacingly at the STUDENT REPORTERS. – STUDENT REPORTERS remain stunned.

66 – INT. SENIOR GIRLS DORMITORY – DAY

CROSS CUT to SENIORS in the dormitory slowly waking up as they appear in wood.

SENIORS 'We can get out'.

They start to cautiously make their escape.

JOSH & CLAIRE 'We have got to stop the union of the SKULLS'.

67 – INT. BREAKFAST ROOM – DAY

JUNIORS 'She's gone – look, we can get out'.

They open the door – they are cautiously free and start to creep out to make an escape. They pass a LARGE POT in the KITCHEN – HEADMASTER STEVE'S HEAD pops out mouthing

HEADMASTER STEVE'S HEAD 'well what do you think I could do with you'. (It is the GODDESS'S voice followed by her inane laughter).

They react, scream etc.

68 – INT. TOP OF THE STAIRS – DAY

SENIORS hearing the noise downstairs, listen intently – they creep further downstairs. The study door is open – it is dark inside – in the middle we see the back of a figure in a hooded cloak – slowly it turns around – the image is of THE GRIM REAPER but with the head of the TRISKAIDEKA CRYSTAL SKULL holding a GLOBE with a bottle instead of a scythe. It is the GODDESS – she roars with a witch's cackle – then vanishes – but returns in the same place – vanishes again but returns. Once again tries to transport but her powers have gone because...

JOSH & CLAIRE 'She can't move – she's drunk!'.

There is an enormous gush of wind through the house.

CLAIRE 'Get the SKULL'

JOSH 'How – it's her head'

CLAIRE 'Rip it off!'.

They both do so – there is an almighty echoing scream – the figure vanishes leaving them holding the SKULL.

69 – EXT. WOOD – DAY

The STUDENT REPORTERS, now alone, still mesmerised, start to get to grips with the situation looking towards the cornfield and start filming and reporting.

70 – CORNFIELD – DAY

The cornfield where the ORB was first found. We see in a circle the SENIOR ALIENS holding up the 12 Skulls above their heads – they vanish – as a flying saucer hovers down and disappears leaving a hurricane force wind in its wake.

71 – CROSS CUTTING – EXT. EDGE OF CORNFIELD – DAY THE STUDENT REPORTERS filming.

THE JUNIORS watching through the hedges. SENIORS watching agog.

STEVE (with the cooking pot on his head) otherwise back to normal watching.

JOSH & CLAIRE holding the TRISKAIDEKA CRYSTAL SKULL.

72 – EXT. EDGE OF CORNFIELD – DAY

We close in on the TRISKAIDEKA CRYSTAL SKULL being held by JOSH & CLAIRE to extreme close up and see it say...

GODDESS'S VOICE 'SOUL – long – got anything for a hangover? Make mine a double'.

Freeze frame.

Credits

THE END

Pronunciation

Tris-kai-dek-a = TRISS-KEY-DECKER

Tris-kai-dek-a-pho-bra = TRISS-KEY-DECKER-PHOBIA

Acknowledgements

Cellar joke by American comedian Emo Philips

Plays: Shakespeare's *A Midsummer Night's Dream*

Edmond Rostand's *Cyrano de Bergerac*

Imagine

Genre: Science Fiction

Casting: 2 – Male/Female – Male/Male – Female/Female

Filming & Acting Challenge:

Special moving image Morphing Effects for the face from human to Alien Grey.

For this publication copyright of the lyrics of each song has been bought.

Copyright of the songs will have to be arranged and bought. If too expensive, source royalty free music, or write your own with suitable lyrics matching the storyline of the lyric in the song being replaced.

Directing this requires building the mystery of the encounter.

Lighting and sound effects will also play a major part in creating the atmosphere.

Additional possibility:

An effect of the space craft disappearing into the distance.

FADE IN

INT. BEDROOM – DAWN

We see an unmade bed. Silence. Then HEAR then see an EARLY MORNING ALARM bedside. Then following in time to the bleep of the alarm flashing pulsating red, green and white light

starts, coming through the window. Then RADIATION INTERFERENCE on the alarm. The lights fade away. Through the window we see...

EX. GARDEN – DAWN

GEORGIA standing in the middle of her garden looking up at the sky. She is disorientated as if she has just been dropped from the sky waving something up there goodbye.

Her short-sleeved nightdress is very obviously on back to front. She has three red diagonal laser cut lines on both of her arms. , Also, laser cuts, in a series on her naked ankles and wrists.

Her feet are bare. She slowly turns to look towards her bedroom window wondering how she got to be where she is.

INT. BEDROOM - DAWN

GEORGIA rushes into her bedroom and immediately picks up a hand mirror and starts to examine marks on her body. She turns the alarm off that is now only making a RADIATION INTERFERENCE NOISE.

As she does so the RADIO turns itself on playing 'The Windmills of Your Mind' sung by Noel Harrison.

> RADIO
> Round like a circle in a spiral, like a wheel within a wheel
>
> Never ending or beginning on an ever spinning reel

She puts the mirror down to search for her watch.

> Like a snowball down a mountain, or a carnival balloon
>
> Like a carousel that's turning running rings around the moon

Finding it she looks at the clock face. We see the hands moving randomly speedily around.

> Like a clock whose hands are sweeping past the minutes of its face

Panicking she is in turmoil as in the following words of the song.

> And the world is like an apple whirling silently in space
>
> Like the circles that you find in the windmills of your mind!

The RADIO stops suddenly at the end of the song. Silence. She picks the mirror up again to examine her face. She sees and we see her reflection in the mirror as the face of an ALIEN GRAY.

At this the RADIO immediately turns on playing Michael Jackson singing 'Man In The mirror'

RADIO

I'm Starting With The Man In The Mirror

I'm Asking Him To Change His Ways

Frightened by what she sees. GEORGIA throws the mirror down. At the same time JO, Georgia's live-in partner, bursts in.

She turns as she watches him grab a holdall and angrily during the next part of the song starts thrusting his belongings into it. GEORGIA is frozen with fear of what she has just seen of herself

And No Message Could Have Been Any Clearer

If You Wanna Make The World A Better Place

(If You Wanna Make The World A Better Place)

Take A Look At Yourself, And Then Make A Change

(Take A Look At Yourself, And Then Make A Change)

(Na Na Na, Na Na Na, Na Na, Na Nah)

At this point in the song JO angrily switches the RADIO off.

JO
Where have you been? Friday night and last night. I've had enough. Who is he?

GEORGIA
Look at me Jo. what do you see?

JO
What do I see? What do I see? A two- timing bitch, that's what I see.

GEORGIA
What day is it?

JO
Time flies when you're enjoying yourself does it? Sunday! Bloody Sunday. Two nights!

GEORGIA

It can't be. It must be Saturday. Help me Jo.

JO

The only thing that can help you is your conscience.

GEORGIA

(Screaming. Crying)

Look at me! Jo they took me.
Look...

She picks up the mirror. Looks into it. We see the ALIEN GREY looking back at her. Jo sees her face in the mirror – no change. She turns to look at him.

Her face is now the ALIEN GREY full onto him. JO passes out. An OVAL BALL OF LIGHT appears above JO. The room fills up with a FOGGY HAZE.

GEORGIA turns slowly back to look at herself in the mirror. Her face in the mirror is now her face as she speaks to it in the mirror.

GEORGIA

(In the mirror face as herself)

We will breed to heel your planet's pain.

She lays the mirror down. The FOG clears and the oval ball of light vanishes from over JO. As she bends down to attend to JO. The RADIO turns on playing John Lennon singing 'Imagine'.

RADIO

Imagine there's no countries
It isn't hard to do
Nothing to kill or die for
And no religion too
Imagine all the people
Living life in peace...
You may say I'm a dreamer
But I'm not the only one
I hope someday you'll join us
And the world will be as one

During the above GEORGIA gets JO into the bed where she joins him. She leans over to kiss him on the last line

'And the world will live as one' ...

GEORGIA
(mouthing)

And the world will live as one

The song stops leaving the RADIO with RADIATION INTERFERENCE NOISE

FADE OUT

Give Peace A Chance

Genre: Murder Detective Drama

Casting: – 3 – 1 Male – 2 Female

Filming & Acting Challenge:

Initially, the audience need to be led to believe the wife/nurse is about to commit suicide.

The suicide note needs to be seen, and printed with the misspelt homophone word 'piece'.

The wife/nurse is a part where the actress is only speaking in the last scene. Great skill is needed in portraying her vulnerability but steely calm in living with her solution to escape her abusive relationship.

When she is ironing she is in control because the ironing board is between her and her husband. In her hand is a deadly weapon, the iron, just in case he attempts to get at her.

The husband is already very drunk when he comes home. His slow burn of insults with gulping down the Lambrini should make it believable that he would pass out in such a short time, especially if in directing his passing out a shot from his POV of the room spinning and his wife going out of focus is included.

A grave in a churchyard should be easily findable that is about 3 months old that has not yet had a headstone put in place. A polite request to the church emphasizing the particular grave will not be identifiable should be made.

The final scene needs to be directed in such a way as to lead the viewer to believe that the wife is going to be arrested for her husband's murder.

The reveal of the wrong homophone word 'piece' as just that, (that is going to be) the evidence that is going to catch her, needs to be seen by the viewer. Some will spot it prior to the Detective pointing it out to the wife.

There needs to be a moment in the direction at the end when the viewer believes the Detective is going to do her duty – then the twist.

Parallel Editing: To build tension a scene of KIERAN leaving a pub and walking home could be inter-cut with JANE's preparations after the audience have discovered it is not JANE who is committing suicide. Will she hide the evidence before he arrives?

FADE IN

INT. BEDSIT – NIGHT

We see a young wife JANE HENSHAW wearing surgical gloves mixing anti-freeze into a bottle of Lambrini. She places the anti-freeze bottle in a cupboard.

On a computer she types

> "I do not wish to be revived. I want to die as I have
> planned in piece."

She presses print. The suicide note emerges from the printer. She takes it and hides it along with the surgical gloves that she takes off once the note is in place.

Looking at her watch we see it reads 10.15pm. She puts up an ironing board, turns some music on and starts to iron her nurse's coat.

A key is heard in the door. It opens with KIERAN her husband struggling in from work drunk, having come from the pub. He throws his coat off.

He goes and turns the music off. Silence.

He struggles to sit at the table.

Then stares as JANE continues to iron while he grabs the bottle of Lambrini, unscrews it and drinks. Then...

KIERAN

(coolly sneering at her)

> You miserable whore. Is there no one you won't look
> at other than me. As soon as my back is turned.

He grabs at the bottle of Lambrini unscrews it and drinks.

> It's you who have driven me to drink. Night nurse...
>
> I love you, but you repay me with deceit. I swear you
> dare humiliate me anymore and I'll kill you!

Holding the bottle towards her threatening to use it against her. Then drinking from it some more in great gulps.

> Kill you – do you hear?

He has finished the bottle. He weakly throws it in her direction as he slumps to the floor, passing out.

Jane stops ironing. Goes to where she put the surgical gloves. Puts them on. Takes the note and squeezes KIERAN'S fingers around it and places it on the table. Takes the anti-freeze bottle out of the cupboard, squeezes his fingers around it and places it on the table. She takes the surgical gloves off and places them in her ironed nurse's coat pocket that she puts on and leaves for her night duty.

EXT. CHURCHYARD – EARLY MORNING

We see JANE HENSHAW in nurses coat after her night shift, laying some flowers with a card among the residue of dead flowers on KIERAN's grave about 3 months after his funeral.

The earth on the grave is still a mound without a headstone. The card is handwritten by Jane and reads

> "We shouldn't have ended like this. Rest in Piece."

We see a WOMAN looking on from a distance.

INT. BEDSIT – EARLY MORNING

A key in the door and JANE enters. She kicks off her shoes. Takes off her coat and hangs it up. There is a KNOCK at the door.

JANE

Who is it?

DETECTIVE ALICE GRIMSHAW

Detective Alice Grimshaw. May I come in?

JANE opens the door. We see it is the WOMAN who was looking on in the graveyard holding out her identity card.

JANE

Yes. Hello. Come in. How can I help you?

DETECTIVE ALICE GRIMSHAW

Your husband's suicide.

249

Pause.

> Your husband had a record before you married him.

JANE

Oh?

DETECTIVE ALICE GRIMSHAW

For domestic abuse. Was he ever abusuve to you?

JANE

No. No. I loved him dearly He never ever behaved badly to me.

DETECTIVE ALICE GRIMSHAW

Why do you think he committed suicide?

JANE

I didn't realise it. We both liked a drink. I think he was an alcoholic. That's what the doctor said.

DETECTIVE ALICE GRIMSHAW

Yes. An alcoholic who added anti- freeze to his drink.

JANE

It poisons a lot of cats.

DETECTIVE ALICE GRIMSHAW

You knowe that?

JANE

Yes. I read it somewhere.

DETECTIVE GRIMSHAW takes from her pocket KIERAN's suicide note that is inside a see-through plastic wallet...

DETECTIVE ALICE GRIMSHAW

Is this the suicide note he printed?

JANE

Yes.

DETECTIVE ALICE GRIMSHAW

It reads "I want to die as I have planned in piece."

DETECTIVE GRIMSHAW takes from her other pocket the card that JANE left with the flowers.

This is the card you left at Kieran's graveside this morning.

You've written "We shouldn't have ended like this. Rest in Piece."

JANE

Yes.

DETECTIVE ALICE GRIMSHAW

Handing JANE the card

I suggest you don't leave anymore cards and destroy this.

DETECTIVE GRIMSHAW takes out a small writing pad and writes

"Give **PEACE** A Chance"

She underlines peace and writes it in uppercase.

She tears it from the pad and hands it to JANE saying out loud

Give 'peace' a chance.

She turns and exits, closing the door behind her.

JANE looks at the Detective's note. Looks at her card.

JANE
(slowly seeing her spelling error)

P-E-A-C-E. PIECE.

Oh – Oh – NO!
(to herself thanking detective, breaking down)

Thank you, Thank you, Thank you, Thank you

FADE OUT

Dice Man

Genre: Murder

Casting: 3 – Male/Male – Female girl as dead body

Filming & Acting Challenge:

Luke Rhinehart (pen name of English Professor George Cockcroft) wrote an excellent book 'Dice Man'. This piece steels the roll of the dice concept from it. Plus it is also loosely based on a true news story of a youth who murdered his girlfriend in exchange for a breakfast in a greasy spoon cafe. So, extraordinary as it may seem, there is a strong thread of truth in this screenplay to make it a successful short film.

The friendship relationship between the two boys will be crucial to making this short film believable. One, Tom, turning out to be a psychopath who frames his best friend.

The audience really need to be made to feel for Henry, having been framed at the end.

All of the premeditated actions Tom frames Henry with will need clever direction so the audience is able to believe that his framing is psychopathically fool-proof.

The wood scene location will be an important character in the story – careful reconnaissance to find a suitable woodland opening where filming without disturbance can take place will be a challenge.

Additional Possibility: a montage at the start of the film of the boys regularly meeting with their friends in a cafe for early breakfast before 6th form.

FADE IN

INT. TOM'S BEDROOM – NIGHT

TOM and HENRY two 16 yr olds are talking

> TOM
> She's pregnant. The problem is I don't know how to
> tell my Mum or her parents or anything. It's hard to,
> because my Mum will be pissed and will kill me and
> if we tell her parents they will kill me too, so either

way I'm dead. So I need a way to tell them both, but in a way they won't kill me. Any good advice?

                    HENRY

Take out a life-insurance policy for yourself Tom. Let them kill you. The payout will pay for her and the baby.

                    TOM

Funny. I'm too young to be a Dad!

Pause.

I've a better idea. I'll kill her and baby.

                    HENRY

Oh – yeah – that's the other side of the coin I suppose – How?

                    TOM
            (Sudden excited idea)

Not a coin. A dice! The 'How' will be decided by a dice.

He goes to a drawer and takes out a dice, grabs a pen and paper. Sits at his desk. Passes the pen and paper to HENRY.

Six numbers. Six ways to do it. The throw of the dice decides. Your writing's easier to read than mine Title it 'The Dice Man'

                    HENRY
        (Amused -playing along with the fantasy)

Ok – Number One – Poison.

HENRY writes.

                    TOM

Two – Push off a cliff.

                    HENRY

Three – Bludgeon with something heavy.

253

                              TOM

Four – Strangle.

                            HENRY

Five – Stab.

                              TOM

Six – Drown.

TOM prepares to throw the dice.

          Here goes...

TOM throws. It comes up with option three.

                            HENRY

Three -

HENRY looks at list.

          Bludgeon with something heavy.

Pause

                              TOM

          Henry – what would you do if I actually did kill her
          and the baby?

HENRY screws the list into a ball and starts to go.

                            HENRY

          Oh – I would buy you breakfast at our favorite
          greasy spoon. See yer...

He throws the list at TOM while letting himself out.

TOM picks up the dice. As he does so a spider crosses the table. He sinisterly bludgeons it several times with a final squash and twist.

EXT. WOOD – DAY

We see TOM burying a pair of blooded gloves. Then we see a hooded girl's body lying curled up on the ground. A rock the size of a rugby ball covered in blood is beside her head. Her handbag is nearby with her mobile phone next to it. We then see TOM standing TEXTING the following.

TEXT

Where are you? Love Tom xxx.

The mobile beside the bag signals receipt of a text. We see

TEXT

Where are you? Love Tom xxx.

HENRY appears.

TOM

What took you so long? You replied to Jane's text asking you to come and meet her here, alone, an hour ago.

HENRY freezes, taking in the scene – then...

Don't say anything, but you may just owe me breakfast.

Pause.

HENRY
(Relieved)

Oh – I see – very funny – the pair of you. You can get up now Jane. You almost got me you...

TOM
(Laughing)

OK – Game's up Jane. Henry look how real that blood on that rock is. Pick it up – lick it – I made it with syrup and red cake die.

HENRY does so laughing. Licks it. Sudden realization – its real blood – throws rock down.

TOM
(Coldly)

Pull back the hood.

HENRY does so. He freezes in disbelief and fear as he stares back at TOM.

She was facing away from you and you thought this is it. You tried to break her neck. She was screaming

so you picked up that rock and started to hit her –
bludgeon – her with it. The worst part was feeling
and seeing her skull give way.

HENRY

You sadistic bastard.

TOM

Murderer! You wrote a list of how you might do it
'Dice Man'. You always fancied her. You thought,
you were in with a chance when she wanted to meet
you here alone. Finding out she was pregnant by
me you ...I followed you here and now I'm going
to tell them what I found. Everything's got your
fingerprints on – the list – the rock the hood.

TOM hurries away repeating, chanting, inanely back.

Everything's got your fingerprints on the list – the
rock – the hood! Everything's got your fingerprints
on – the list – the rock – the hood!

Chanting echoing fading away.

Wooded stillness. Henry stands frozen, tears streaming down his face.

FADE OUT

Fingerprints

Genre: Detective Murder

Casting: 2 – Male/Male – Female/Female – Male/Female

Filming & Acting Challenge:

The Son/Daughter answering the Detective's questions, has the difficult job of describing the murder scene for the audience whilst bringing to the fore their backstory of the relationship with their father.

The detective controls the conversation, leading to the revelation of who the murderer was.

Filming this will benefit from an authentic vicarage study location.

The audience need to be drawn in by the camera's prying inquisition from the Detective's point of view.

Plenty of reaction shots of the Detective will break the length of the Son/Daughter's dialogue.

Then, of course, a POV of the Phone at the crucial point.

FADE IN

INT. STUDY – DAY

We see a DETECTIVE questioning JAMES STADDON, the son of the murder victim.

> DETECTIVE
> I know this must be very difficult for you James.
> Having found your father only a few days ago in
> this very room – murdered.

> JAMES
> It's your job Detective. I've seen enough TV
> programmes to know that immediate family are the
> first suspects. So ask what you need.

DETECTIVE

Well, I need you to once again describe to me how you found your father.

Pause

JAMES

I knocked on the door. Dad always insisted on that ever since I could walk. I learnt my lesson when I was 5. It was also the start of my being educated in his colourful vocabulary – something I'm sure many of his adoring congregation would be shocked at if they knew how frequently his abusive language permeated these walls. St. Michael Staddon he certainly was not – but I – loved him as Dad being Dad. Not Bishop Staddon orator of famed philosophical sermons that he penned in this very study.

Pause

I'm not sure he even believed in God. You see his beloved wife had died in childbirth – my birth – my mother. It would have been a bad career move to throw God out with my bathwater – so 5 years later we were moved into this house with him having risen in the ranks inheriting this bishopric.

DETECTIVE

James – you're still outside the door.

JAMES

Yes – sorry. Perhaps I don't want to go in.

Pause

You see – there not being an answer after my third knock – I did indeed risk the wrath of God by opening the door aware that waking him up if he had nodded off could ignite an incendiary volley of abuse that could bring back my childhood memories of inconsolable wailing at the hurt of it all.

However I needed to ask him a most pressing question – but I digress.

There he was. The french window behind him open. Curtain billowing in the breeze. Dad inert, thrust forward across his desk dribbling blood. I at first wanted to run. But thought as it looked as if he had had a heart attack that perhaps I could give him the kiss of life. So I rushed forward – but then – but then stopped shocked – because there between his shoulder blades sticking out from his back was – was the knife that your Forensics took away as the murder weapon.

Pause

DETECTIVE

Then – what did you do next James?

JAMES

Well of course what else could I do? I dialed 999 instantly.

The murderer might be waiting to get me. I was frozen to the spot. The phone on Dad's desk was immediately to hand – so I phoned, scared out of my wits.

DETECTIVE

This phone here?

He walks to the phone and points at it.

JAMES

Yes.

Pause

DETECTIVE

There were no fingerprints on the murder weapon.

JAMES

The murderer is not going to be that stupid is he? He'd wear gloves.

259

DETECTIVE

Yes. You would wouldn't you James?

JAMES

Yes.

Pause

DETECTIVE

Your Dad's fingerprints were on the receiver.

JAMES

Of course – he was the only person who used that phone.

DETECTIVE

Except of course you – when you dialled 999.

JAMES

Yes.

Pause

DETECTIVE

You didn't take the gloves off.

JAMES

What?

Pause

DETECTIVE

You didn't take the gloves off.

Pause

Your fingerprints are not on the phone.

James looks dumbfounded.

FADE OUT

Entrapment

Genre: Romantic Drama

Casting: 1 Male 1 Female – Waiter/Waitress – Crowd

Filming and Acting Challenge:

Filming at a crowded location will require location releases/permissions and health and safety vigilance to avoid causing danger to any member of the public. If a member of the public is recognisable in a shot, a release form will have to be signed. Best to have some extras (family and friends) to make up immediate background talent.

The audience must not think that the WOMAN sees the MAN with her purse-wallet. They do need to clock her glancing at him and note that she sees him with his wallet and where he puts it.

The audience does see the WOMAN take his wallet. Because they are sitting so close together the audience will accept that she was able to get it without being noticed.

The two leading characters need to have chemistry between them so that we believe the relationship could develop as scripted.

An alternative ending is obvious – I was in two minds – your choice. WOMAN can be either a real Detective with it ending at her looking at her phone or a Con Artist as it is concluded.

FADE IN

INT. RAILWAY CONCOURSE – DAY

It is busy. We see a MAN approach a WOMAN who is standing around looking at her mobile. Her bag is precariously vulnerable to what happens next.

MAN slips his hand in the bag and takes out her purse- wallet. He quickly walks a distance away opening it. He takes out some assorted notes £20 – £10 etc. He closes the purse- wallet propping it under his arm pit while taking out his own wallet that we see clearly as he puts his ill gotten gains into it. We see the WOMAN briefly glancing over at him as he holds his wallet.

She sees him put his wallet back into his outside overcoat pocket, before looking away. Taking the WOMAN'S purse- wallet from under his arm pit he holds it looking back at the WOMAN.

She is good looking so he decides to try his luck. Walking towards her he drops her purse wallet on the ground by her and...

MAN

Excuse me. Is this yours?

Having picked up her wallet.

WOMAN

Oh!

She rummages in her bag. Realising...

Yes, How did that happen? It must have fallen out when I took my phone out.

Thank you. Thank you.

MAN

I know how that feels. Luckily someone found mine a few months back – no address in it – so they used my bank account details on the debit card putting one penny into the account that allowed 18 characters to write a message. I FOUND YOUR, then another penny, WALLET IN THE ROAD, and another penny, TEXT OR CALL, so with the fourth penny their contact details.

WOMAN

Ingenious

MAN

Lucky. An honest dude. I bought him a bottle of wine.

WOMAN

Oh. The least I can do is buy you a coffee. Have you got time?

MAN

Good idea.

WOMAN

Long as you are not in a hurry to get somewhere?

MAN

Always in a hurry. But yes, coffee is a good idea.

They walk towards a sit in restaurant bar.

INT. RESTAURANT BAR – DAY

Sitting down. It is crowded so they have to sit next to each other at a table. Man takes his overcoat off and drapes over chair.

WOMAN

What do you do?

MAN

Oh – This and That.

WOMAN

Well THAT is very clear if its THIS!

Both laugh. WAITRESS comes over

MAN

What do you want?

WOMAN

Cappuccino please.

MAN

I'll have the same – thank you.

WAITRESS goes.

MAN

To be more specific – software – I've got my own software company.

> WOMAN

Oh?

> MAN

Yes. I've just got back from Florence on business where I was also able to take my 14 year old daughter who is studying the renaissance. A little treat for her to help 'up' her GCSE grades. I got custody after her mum got put into prison for 4 years.

> WOMAN

Oh dear – sorry to hear that. What for?

> MAN

Fraud. She's an an accountant, was an accountant. Earning a lot more than me. Now I know why.

Both laugh. WAITRESS arrives with coffee.

> WOMAN

Evan so. You did well to get custody. She must have been bad. Most men lose out making it difficult over time to maintain a relationship with their children.

> MAN

Well – it wasn't hard to show that she was cracked.

Pause

> WOMAN

So – a bottle of wine Eh?

> MAN

Oh – yes – well not much really for all the time it would have taken cancelling all of my credit cards and waiting for renewals.

> WOMAN

O.M.G. that's what I would have had to do had you not found my purse.

MAN

Bit of luck I went to my account to make sure I wasn't already being cleaned out.

WOMAN

Just shows you can never be too careful – unlike me today.

MAN

Yes well – there you are.

WOMAN
(flirtatiously)

Yes here I am.

Pause

Soft-ware eh?. Soft Ware – always makes me think of lingerie.

MAN
(flirting back)

Really? Could always do with some good solid Hard Ware to complement it.

WOMAN

Like this.

Taking mobile out of her bag.

Let me take a picture.

MAN

Don't pull your wallet out with it again.

WOMAN

No.

Getting in close to him and Taking a selfie of them both. Showing picture.

MAN

We make a good couple.

WOMAN

As long as I'm not cracked. THIS could
be my lucky day.

MAN

And THAT with me already having found
your wallet.

WOMAN

THIS and THAT

MAN

A working day with benefits?

Signalling to waitress. The next step could be a hotel room.

I'll pay.

WAITRESS arrives with paper bill on silver tray. MAN goes to take out his wallet.

MAN

Oh – I er...

Rifling through his pockets. First one then the other.

I seem to have lost it!

WOMAN

I said I would pay.

MAN

No – you don't understand – I've
really lost my wallet!

WOMAN

And I said I would pay.

She takes out from her bag his wallet – finding a £10 note that she puts on the tray.

To waitress

Keep the change.

WAITRESS goes.

> MAN

That's my wallet!

> WOMAN

Typical man. You talked about yourself but never asked what I did for a living. Not that anything you said other than THIS and THAT was true.

So what could I be? Hustler? Jewellery thief? Accountant?

Or

A night-mare

> MAN

Cracked.

> WOMAN

No

She shows him her Police ID.

> MAN

No benefits?

> WOMAN

No benefits P P P Pick pocketing pick pocketer.

Holding out rest of notes from his wallet.

> Every one marked.

He gets up to go.

> Sit down. CCTV remember...

He sits back down.

> Plus...

She takes her mobile out again and looks at the picture of them both.

Shame, we did make a good looking couple – but sadly you're a marked man.

Unless

Pause

This

Taking out her ID again

Is a fake

Man takes it and looks closer. Looks up.

MAN

Done over!

FADE OUT

Will They Or Won't They?

Genre: Romantic Comedy

Casting: 2 – Female/Male – Party Guests

Filming & Acting Challenge:

The actors need to have chemistry between them. The audience must believe that they fancy each other.

This piece requires clear spoken delivery and comic timing.

Directing this you will have the challenge of getting your actors to have business to do/reactions when not speaking while the thoughts of each are being relayed to the audience.

POV's of the other partygoers will help.

Explore the embarrassing silences in the conversation. Someone could come by with a tray of canapes on offer etc. to break the gaps.

Possible Addition:

Cut after a lengthy pause at the end to:

Tasteful passionate lovemaking.

Did they or didn't they? Was it in their minds?

Titles...

Plus – Break the Fourth Wall?

Instead of the CONCIENCE of both characters being voiced, it would be interesting to see how it would work with both characters speaking directly to camera at those points.

FADE IN

INT. FLAT – DAY

It's JANET'S birthday. A small get together includes KIERAN standing to one side holding some idle chat. The door bell rings. JANET goes and opens the door. It's vivacious atractive GILLY who high heels in.

JANET

Gilly. Hooray.

KIERAN watches GILLY as she gives a present to Janet.

KIERAN CONSCIENCE

Ah, Gilly – that's her name. Acted together in bit parts in that brilliant short film 4 yrs ago. She's looking good. Fancied her then. But I was with Karen. Now though...

GILLY turns around catches sight of KIERAN.

KIERAN

Hello. How are you Gilly?

KIERAN CONSCIENCE

She'll like me remembering her name.

GILLY

Oh. Hello. Yeah good – and you?

GILLY CONSCIENCE

What's his name? James. No, that was the character he played in that terrible short film we were in.

KIERAN

Things are going well.

KIERAN CONSCIENCE

Things couldn't be worse.

GILLY

What are you doing now?

GILLY CONSCIENCE

Is it Coren ?

KIERAN

Writing – not acting anymore.

KIERAN CONSCIENCE

That can be why she hasn't seen me in anything recently.

GILLY CONSCIENCE

Probably best. He wasn't that good apart from his looks. Yeah, good looking and not gay.

Better let him know I have a husband now. Wave the ring around.

GILLY

Are you writing a screen play?

KIERAN

Poetry.

KIERAN CONSCIENCE

What a lie. But a chance to hook her with a little 'Crowing' from my favourite Ted Hughes poem...

GILLY CONSCIENCE

Didn't expect that.

GILLY

Romantic.

KIERAN

Yes – well it can be. I'm more Ted Hughes than Keats. Less ethereal More earthy.

"He loved her and she loved him. His kisses sucked out her whole past and future or tried to. He had no other appetite...

GILLY

"She bit him. She gnawed. She sucked." I love Ted Hughes!

GILLY CONSCIENCE

He tricked me. He's dangerous. Don't flirt.

KIERAN CONSCIENCE

Good quote. She knew it "She bit him, she gnawed, she sucked" With me, any day, any night – yes – come on – I'm in!

GILLY

Sylvia Plath and him – so romantic – two great poets marrying – tragic she committed suicide.

KIERAN

Yes – they think now she was bipolar.

GILLY CONSCIENCE

I don't remember him being so knowledgeable and sensitive. Is it Kayly ? No don't don't want to know. I've got to get away from him. He's really very, very, very...

KIERAN CONSCIENCE

She's mirroring me. Copying my hand movements.

GILLY

My husband doesn't like poetry.

GILLY

There. That's it I've mentioned him. I'm safe.

KIERAN CONSCIENCE

Oh no. Husband. Left hand – there it is – the ring on the finger. Must remember to look! Don't show her you've been wasting your time trying to chat her up. Wind up and move on...

KIERAN

How long have you been married?

GILLY

3 yrs. He's on a bicycle road race at the moment. That's why he's not here.

GILLY CONSCIENCE

He's never here. Always riding the bloody bicycle.
Wish he'd ride me a bit more often!

GILLY

We're both health freaks. He's down the gym twice
a day. I run every day. It's so relaxing.

KIERAN CONSCIENCE

Bet the sex is good. Stop it! Wasting your time.
Move on.

KIERAN

Don't over-do it. You must both be exhausted.

KIERAN CONSCIENCE

I'd love to exhaust you but not in the gym. She's so
gorgeous. Go on, husband's not here – she may be
up for playing away...

KIERAN

Got to be careful with cycling. They say it can effect
your sperm count.

GILLY CONSCIENCE

I've told him that! I bet Colin's – no what is his name –
I bet his count is good. Got to get away. Dangerous.

GILLY

Not ready for kids yet.

GILLY CONSCIENCE

I'm desperate to start. Maybe he has been firing
blanks? Kieran – its Kieran.

GILLY

Kieran what about you. Have you got any?

KIERAN CONSCIENCE

She remembers my name. She wouldn't have done
that if she didn't fancy me.

KIERAN

If I had found someone like you

I'd love to have done. But not so far.

GILLY CONSCIENCE

That's it – help.

GILLY

Oh that's sweet of you to say. I'm married remember?

KIERAN

Sadly yes.

KIERAN CONSCIENCE

She's hooked. I'll give her my killer look. Both of my eyes to each one of hers.

GILLY CONSCIENCE

How can I resist those eyes. He's being so attentive.

KIERAN

Good to see you again.

GILLY

You too.

KIERAN

Sorry your husband doesn't like poetry.

KIERAN CONSCIENCE

Come on Ted " She wanted him complete inside her"

GILLY CONSCIENCE

"She wanted him complete inside her".

Awkward, lingering, longing, silence.

FADE OUT

As Good As Gold

Genre: Comic Drama

Casting: 2 male 1 Female

Filming and Acting Challenge:

All three characters need to have charm. The WOMAN and MAN sex-appeal and chemistry between them.

Directing this piece: reaction shots, pace and tension have to be skillfully handled. Tension between the characters when they reveal their dissembling needs to leave the audience believing the next move until it quickly changes.

Lighting will be essential to create the atmosphere from dusk to night in a graveyard.

Realistic props for the gold bars will require accurate research and propmaking. Possibly only two bars need to be made.

FADE IN

EXT. RURAL RAILWAY STATION – DUSK

We see a couple in their twenties. The WOMAN is marching with some urgency towards the MAN. She is holding a gun to his body, hidden by her coat that is slung between them over their linked arms. We see the gun (passers-by would not).

A DRIVER late 30's is slowly moving his parked car to leave when the WOMAN opens the rear nearside door and pushes the MAN in, sliding in behind him shutting the door behind her and pointing the gun at the DRIVER'S head.

INT. CAR – DUSK

                    WOMAN
          Drive!

The DRIVER slowly starts to move off saying...

                    DRIVER
          That's not a real gun.

The WOMAN points the gun at the front passenger seat floor and fires a shot.
SFX: BANG

OK. It's a real gun.

A PEDESTRIAN catches the DRIVER'S eye from the off-side in shock. The Driver whose window is open, covers by smiling and shouting

Backfire!

Where are we going?

WOMAN

I don't know.

To MAN

Where are we going?

MAN

I suppose you want to go to where it is?

WOMAN

Yes. Where is it?

DRIVER

Can you make up your minds? There's a crossroads ahead.

MAN

Turn right.

DRIVER

Who's your lady friend?

MAN

Allow me to introduce you – this is my wife Alison. Ali when on more friendly terms. Take the next left.

DRIVER

Very romantic.

MAN

It was – we met on my yacht in the Caribbean. This little darling here was my armed bodyguard.

DRIVER

So...she's for real.

WOMAN

Yes. I'm for real. Drive.

MAN

Straight ahead.

DRIVER

Kinky!

MAN

Perhaps that was the attraction... but at this moment...the fear factor has rendered me completely impotent.

DRIVER

You and me both. Do you have to keep pointing that thing at us?

WOMAN

At least you now both know what its like to have something hard pointing at you when you're not in the mood.

DRIVER

Oh dear. You must have really upset her. I've heard of money can't buy you love – but this is ridiculous. Did you lose it all?

MAN

No. But it looks as if I'm about to. Pull up on the left there please. Divorce. Ali wants the money. Ali- mony.

The car pulls up and stops.

                    WOMAN
          This is a graveyard.

                     MAN
          All good things must come to an end.

                    DRIVER
          Well. Count me out of it – I'm not good!

                    WOMAN
          Shut up. Give me the keys.

DRIVER hands her the keys.

          Now. Where is it?

                     MAN
          You'd better follow me.

                    WOMAN
          Ok. Both get out.

EXT. CAR – NIGHT

WOMAN opens nearside door quickly and covers exterior of car with gun. MAN opens offside back door gets out. DRIVER gets out. MAN walks through church yard gate.

EXT. CHURCHYARD – NIGHT

WOMAN follows covering with gun DRIVER and MAN who is leading.

                    DRIVER
          Look. I'm no marriage guidance counsellor. So
          I don't see how I can help you. Perhaps I'll go now?

MAN stops by a newly interred grave that as yet has no headstone, only a temporary plaque in the ground. The earth is mounded 10 inches above in the shape of the coffin below.

                     MAN
          As I said 'all good things must come to an end'.

DRIVER

DRIVER bends down and reads name on plaque
James Owen 1979-2015.

MAN

Shame he had to die. I was rather close to him. Not
many others were. Only the 4 pall-bearers at his
funeral to carry the coffin, attended.

DRIVER

DRIVER scrapes away some earth to reveal a Kilo Gold Bar. Standing up to MAN
holding bar.

So at last we meet, James. Dead man walking.

MAN

What? Who are you?

DRIVER

Tell him.

WOMAN

Sorry James. Our driver today is Detective Inspector
Tim from the Fraud Squad.He's my boss. I started
investigating your lucrative internet frauds when first
sent to guard you over 2 happy years of marriage
ago.

DRIVER

Your own death certificate – just another string to
your bow. Luckily you loved the honey I sent you.

MAN

And now the trap is complete?

Pause.

Pass me the gun honey.

WOMAN passes him the gun.

And yours Tim.

WOMAN takes it off him and keeps it.

> Perhaps you'd be kind enough to help us load your car with – how many bars did I say darling? 95 One Kilo bars of gold in the coffin. I think that's how much it weighed when put in the ground. And a little extra on top. Over £25,000 a bar.

> WOMAN
> Sorry Tim. My cover was blown soon after we started dating. Honey trap to head-over-heels love-trap.

> DRIVER
> Well, I'm very pleased to see it. You see, James and I went to the same school. We struck a masonic deal. I'd get our department off his back for a 'reasonable return'.

> Only you as the only other person aware of his activities were so fired- up to make your first big catch, we had to test your commitment against your oath of departmental honesty and your proclamation of 'til death us do part' honey vows.

> It seems she really does love you James.Not so sure on what she was planning on doing with me.

Picking up a bar of gold,

> Her record said she was as good as gold, and she's proved it!

WOMAN grabs gun from MAN and now holds a gun in each hand.

> WOMAN
> You bastards! You were both in on this from the beginning? Sorry boys. But I'm not a member of any masonic lodge. I think I deserve all of this to be all mine. Now, tell me, why shouldn't I kill you both?

Threatening both of them. A gun in each hand.

                              MAN
It is quite heavy.

                             WOMAN
A reasonable return?

                             DRIVER
Yes. I return and close this investigation as
inconclusive because James died. Work a few more
years and retire early for my 'reasonable return'.
(Which I am sure even you would prefer to give
me, rather than draw attention to a shot body in a
grave yard).

DRIVER takes guns from her.

EXT. YACHT - SUNSET

We see MAN and WOMAN cuddled together drinking champagne on yacht.

                            DRIVER V.O
You sail away into the sunset with a new 'til death
us do part' identity. You having gone for a long
swim out to sea leaving a suicide note unable to
cope with the sad loss of your first husband. Who
I am sure before his passing has also graciously
created a death certificate for your demise.

Perhaps I should take up marriage guidance.

                              MAN
I knew he wouldn't let me down. At school we were
as thick as thieves.

I had to be sure about you though, but

you were...

                             WOMAN
As good as gold?

                                              FADE OUT

Slave Girl

Genre: Docudrama

Cast: 3 - White MISTRESS 35+. White MASTER 45+. Black 16 year old IDA.

Filming challenge: This script is loosely based on an excerpt from Harriet Jacobs's autobiography *Incidents in the Life of a Slave Girl* published in 1861. It is a book I urge all to read to discover the ignominy of slavery in America prior to that time.

Historical: accuracy needs to be researched; set, costume, make-up and etiquette.

Casting: use type casting as near to the following... MISTRESS is a 'totally deficient in energy' American Southern Belle; from a life of being served and children wet nursed. MASTER is an evil looking white American South plantation owning louche. He needs to make women's skin crawl with his lascivious manner towards IDA.

IDA: is a negro slave. She was bequeathed to her MASTER at the age of nine by his elder sister. In her household she had gleaned a modicum of reading and writing by being on occasion with her children when serving them.

She is pretty. However, she needs to look skinny. She needs to look unfed...slaves received throughout the year a weekly ration of corn and bacon often with the unwelcome added protein of maggots. Other nutrients needed to be stolen.

Directing: this piece will require the camera to be each character's eyes letting the viewer experience the pain of IDA's existence.

Actors: all of the characters need a period version of a Southern American accent. Be aware that with an accent not your own you may be speaking louder than usual. Tone it down.

Fight direction: The BLOW needs to be truly shocking - such that it could have really killed her.

FADE IN

EXT. SECLUDED AMERICAN SOUTH PLANTATION HOUSE GARDEN - DAY

We see IDA and her MISTRESS in confrontation hidden away from prying eyes

                        IDA

Missus. He is a carpenter, a free-born coloured
man. He wants to buy my freedom from you and
the massa so we can marry.

                    MISTRESS

Do you suppose that I will have you tending my
children with the children of a negro? I'll have you
peeled with the whip and, pickled in salt aft, to
heal the lacerations that will deservedly double the
pain - if I ever hear you mention this subject again.

She goes to strike her but pulls back then says the following with quiet sinister
jealous relish...

Your job in life is to have no family ties of your
own. You were created to wait upon my family -
alone. That is why that mulatto child you bore your
master was buried, by you, after you snuffed its life
out to hide the disgusting shame of having opened
your black legs to him.

She pauses enjoying the profound hurt her jealousy inflicts on IDA. We see IDA
numb with the painful memory.

Yes I knew, and for that - you pretty little thing - you
shall never leave my sight. From tonight onwards,
you are to sleep on the floor outside my room as a
good dog does with its owner.

                        IDA

She is in heaven.

                    MISTRESS

Heaven! There is no such place for a bastard!

IDA cries out in tears and pain. MISTRESS grabs at IDA's hair twisting a hold
on her.

You suffer do you? I am glad of it. You deserve it
all, and more too.

MISTRESS lets go and leaves. IDA is left alone. Broken.

EXT. MISTRESS'S BEDROOM DOOR - NIGHT

We see IDA arriving outside her MISTRESS's door. She curls up on the bare floor with nothing but a blanket to cover her.

Closes her eyes to sleep.

INT. MISTRESS'S BEDROOM - NIGHT

We see MISTRESS open her door, glance at IDA with satisfaction. Then we see her getting into her comfortable bed with the MASTER asleep beside her.

EXT. MASTER'S STUDY - FOLLOWING MORNING

The door is open as IDA approaches. Through it she sees her odious MASTER sitting at his desk. She stands in trepidation for a while before entering.

INT. MASTER'S STUDY - FOLLOWING MORNING

MASTER stands from his desk, walks around IDA his slave girl, eying his property in disdainful lascivious silence; finally shutting the door and returning to his seat.

> MASTER
>
> I needed to speak with you because of what you
> informed your mistress of yesterday.

Pause.

> I have half a mind to kill you on the spot.

EXT. MASTER'S STUDY - MORNING

We see the MISTRESS now listening at the door. INT. MASTER'S STUDY - MORNING

> So you want to be married, do you? And to a free man.

> IDA

Yes sir.

> MASTER
>
> Well now. It seems, I and your mistress need to
> convince you of who you are beholden to. Either it
> is us, or the negro puppy you honour so highly.

IDA

You promised to treat me well.

MASTER

You have let your tongue run too far; damn you!

IDA

She knew about the baby being yours; but not from me. You know, that I know, that it would have been a crime, for a slave to tell who the father is. She hates me for what you did to me. You sir, hate me for destroying your property. But I could not bear to see a girl child, your bastard, born into slavery - to have my life - to see her torn from me when old enough, to see her dragged away by the highest bidder, screaming, to know her owner would be her abuser, as you to me.

The MASTER coldly ignores IDA's proclamation.

MASTER

If you must have a husband, you may take up with one of your fellow slaves here on the plantation.

IDA

Being another of your slaves, he would have no law to protect me from your disgusting pleasure - married or not.

EXT. MASTER'S STUDY - MORNING

The MISTRESS intent on the conversation.

INT. MASTER'S STUDY - MORNING

Do you suppose sir, that I being a slave, have no feelings of preference for the kind of man I should Marry? Do you suppose that all men are alike to a slave girl?

MASTER

Do you love this - this free born negro?

IDA

Yes sir.

MASTER

How dare you tell me so!

EXT. MASTER'S STUDY - MORNING

The MISTRESS pleased at her husband's displeasure.

INT. MASTER'S STUDY - MORNING

I supposed you thought more of yourself, that you felt above the insults of such puppies.

IDA

If he is a puppy I am a puppy, for we are both of the negro race. It is right and honourable for us to love each other. The man you call a puppy never insulted me, sir. Never gave me a mulatto baby.

At this the MASTER leaps at her giving her a stunning BLOW. She almost falls to the ground knocked out, recovering she mouths

You struck me for answering you honestly. So, honestly also know this; I despise you!

EXT. MASTER'S STUDY - MORNING

The MISTRESS delighted at all of what she is hearing.

INT. MASTER'S STUDY - MORNING

Silence. A long silence between them both. As IDA recovers from having been struck with such vengeance and the MASTER deciding on the further punishment he can inflict on his chattel for such insolence.

MASTER

Do you know what you have said?

IDA

Yes, sir, but your treatment drove me to it.

MASTER

Do you know that I have a right to do as I like with you - that I can kill you, if I please?

IDA

You near killed me when you struck me, and I wish you had, because living, you have no right to do what you like with me...

MASTER

Silence! By heaven, girl you forget yourself too far.

IDA

Heaven? By Heaven? If there is a Heaven take me there...

IDA proffers her body and face towards the MASTER begging him to strike her again.

for sure as you stand there a Christian - you are the Devil and this is Hell!

MASTER

Are you mad?

Silence. Long pause.

Do you think any other master would have borne this from you without killing you on the spot? But, death after what you have said to me, would be too kind. Jail would be more becoming of your insolence, don't you think?

IDA

There would be more peace there than there is here.

MASTER

You deserve to go there. To be under such treatment, that you would forget the meaning of the word peace. It would do you good. It would take some of your high notions out of you.

But I am not ready to send you there yet, notwithstanding your ingratitude for all my kindness and forbearance. You have been the plague of my life. I have wanted to make you happy, and I have been repaid with the basest ingratitude; but though you have proved yourself incapable of appreciating my kindness, I will be lenient towards you, Ida.

I will give you one more chance to redeem your character. If you behave yourself and do as I require, I will forgive you and treat you as I always have done; but if you disobey me, I will punish you as I would the meanest slave on my plantation.

Never let me hear that fellow's name mentioned again. If I ever know of you speaking to him, I will cowhide you both; and if I catch him lurking about my premises, I will shoot him as I would a dog. Do you hear what I say? I'll teach you a lesson about marriage and free negroes. Now go, and let this be the last time I have occasion to speak to you on this subject.

IDA opens the door and leaves.

EXT. MASTER'S STUDY - MORNING

We see the MISTRESS having stood away. IDA walks past her in a trance like state not seeing her, tears streaming down her face

IDA

(from under her breath we hear)

I want a free family. A free family away from this atmosphere of hell. Please God if you are there...

INT. MASTER'S STUDY - MORNING

The MISTRESS walks in. Closes the door. Confronts her husband.

MISTRESS

"I will be lenient with you Ida".

MASTER

As I to you. Will she not be a good wet nurse?

He gently puts his hand on her stomach. They kiss.

FADE TO BLACK

Appendix 1

CAST LIST
(THIS IS CONFIDENTIAL INFORMATION ONLY
THE PRODUCTION MANAGER ONLY)

Date		Page 1 of 1
16th November		
Production Company	Production Title	Prod. Manager.

Mirror Up To Nature
Abby Singer

How To...

Character	Cast no.	Name and Address	Telephone Number
The Hat	3	James Abbott 16 Lime Grove Edisole Brickshire BK1 1SA	0208 986784
The Sting	5	Bria Adesola Southhaven devon DS4 8PQ	8679234862

CREW LIST

**(CHECK - CONFIDENTIAL INFORMATION FOR PRODUCTION TEAM
ONLY BUT IT MAYBE INCLUDED IN THE WELCOME PACK
GIVEN OUT TO CREW BUT NOT ALL CREW MAY WANT THEIR
HOME ADDRESSES GIVEN OUT).**

Date   Page of

Production Company   Production Title   Prod. Manager.

Position	Name and Address	Telephone Number

Talent CALL SHEET NO....1..of......1...

PRODUCTION COMPANY: Mirror Up To Nature	
Film: How To	Date 16th November
Director: Mac Guffin	Unit Call 6.30 am
Producer: I Amboss	Costume 6.30 am
Production Manager: Abby Singer	Make-Up 7.am
	Weather Report
	Sunrise/Sunset

PRODUCTION OFFICE	UNIT OFFICE
10 Wardour Street London W1 Tel: 030 003492	

LOCATION/STUDIO	Location Contact:
Pinewood	Abby Singer 0278923

Sets	Sc. No.	D/N	I/E	Pages	Location	Synopsis	Cast No.
Gambling Den	8	N	I	2. 2/8	Studio 3	The stakes are high - fight and shooting	1 & 2

No.	Cast	Character	Pick/Up	W/R M/U	On Set
3	James Abbott	The Hat	5am	6.30	7.45
5	Bria Adesola	The Sting	5.30am	6.30	7.45

Shooting Schedule - Day One

Production Company: Mirror Up To Nature   **Film Title:** How To.........

Director: K.N. Owhow

Location: House

Sheet No: 1 of 1

Date: 16/04

Total Time: 6Hrs

Scenes: 8/10/20

Wednesday September 18th |

Full Cast & Crew - 7am

SCENE	INT/ EXT	DAY/ NIGHT	PAGE LENGTH	SET & PROPS	CHARACTERS	MAKE-UP	WARDROBE	LOCATION
8	INT	DAY	4/8	Kitchen - Flat Screen Television with Smashed screen - Spilled broken coffee mug having been thrown at it	1 & 2	1 with bruised face	1 & 2 torn clothing	26 Redland Rd Liverpool LM4 4SA
10	INT	DAY	3/8	Bedroom - unmade double bed - Bedside picture with smashed frame and glass	1			
20	INT	DAY	2/8	Garage - car with engine running - Door closed - windows of car shut - Hose pipe	2	Asphyxiated look		

Equipment:

Shot List

Sheet No: 1
Date: 16/04
Total Time: 6Hrs

Production Title: How To...
Director: K.N. Owhow
Location: House

Scenes: 8/10/--

Scene	Camera Position	Shot Size	Movement	Equipment	Location	Ext/Int D/N	Character	Notes
8	A	Master	Static	Kit: a - b - c	Kitchen	Int	1 & 2	Make sure a still is taken
	B	MCU					1	of each room
	B	CU					1	prior to moving
	C	MCU					2	furniture - so that
	C	CU					2	location can be left as
10	A	Master	Static	Kit: a - b - c	Bedroom	Int	1	we found it.
	B	MCU					1	
	B	CU					1	
20	A	Master	Dolly	Kit: a - b - c	Garage	Int	2	
	B	ECU	Static				2	

Production Company: Mirror Up To Nature

Risk Assessment

Location: Kitchen - 26 Redland Rd - Liverpool LM14 4SA   Film Title| How to........   Sheet..1..of...1

Hazard reference

(a) Confined Spaces	(b) Falls from Height	c) Striking by mobile platform	(d) Trip or Slip	(e) Collapse	f) Manual Handling	(g) Electrical	(h) Hazardous Substances	(i) Noise & Vibration	(j) Fire	(k) Explosion	(L) Others	(m) Others

Severity (S)

1. Negligable - all in a days work
2. Minor - minor injury with short term effect
3. Severe - major injury/disability (reportable)
4. Extreme - fatal

Likelihood (L)

1. Improbable
2. Remote - unlikely
3. Possible - may or could well occur
4. Probable - expected to occur several times

Risk Factor (R)   S x L = R

= 4 Risk may need to be controlled - LOW
= 4 - 6 Risk must be controlled - MEDIUM
= 7 - 9 Hazard must be controlled - HIGH
= 9 + Hazard must be avoided - VERY HIGH

Hazard ref	Hazard Description	People at risk	Initial Assessment S	L	R	Control Measures	Controlled Risk S	L	R	Action Comments
e	Lights and cables	All	3	3	9	Equipment must have been PAT tested - only Gaffer & Best Boy & assistants to handle - extension leads unwound - no excessive load on drawn from one room that will be looped.	2	2	4	Make sure cables are gaffered down

Completed by ....   Date ....   Copies to ....

Reviewed by ....   Review Date (s)

Budget

N.B 30% price mark up is applied if working for a client

Working Title	How to...
Production Company	Mirror Up To Nature
Production No:	1

Item	NO of	DAYS/HRS	Unit Cost	Cost	Price 30% See N.B	Actual Cost
1) Above the line costs						
A Story/Script/Development				£1,100	£1,430	£800
B Producers fee				£4,000	£5,200	£4,000
Directors fee				£4,000	£5,200	£4,000
E Principle artists						
Total 'above the line' cost				**£9,100**	**£11,830**	**£8,800**
2) Below the line costs						
C **Salaries**						
1 Production manager	1	14 days	£100	£1,400	£1,820	£1,400
2 Script Superviser / Continuity	1	14 days	£80	£1,120	£1,456	£1,120
3 Camera crew/DP	1	5 days	£150	£750	£976	£750
4 Gaffer	1	5 days	£150	£750	£976	£750
5 Sound/Boom operator	1	5 days	£100	£500	£650	£600
6 Make-up artist/Hairdresser	1	5 days	£70	£350	£455	£350
7 On line editor	1	5 days	£150	£750	£975	£750
D **Salaries**						
1 Art department graphics	1	1 day	£200	£200	£260	£250
E Artistes						
1 Presenter	1	5 days	£200	£1,000	£1,300	£1,250
2 Actress	1	2 days	£100	£200	£260	£200
F Music Copywrite			£150	£150	£195	£150
G Costume/wigs	2		£100	£200	£260	£200
H Misc. production stores						
I Cards	2		£13	£156	£203	£100
J Studio/editing rentals	1	3 days	£150	£450	£585	
K Equipment		5 days		£1,500	£1,950	
L Power		5 days			£200	£150
M Travel & Transport		5 days		£500	£650	£650
N Hotel & Living expenses				£1,500	£1,950	£1,500
O Insurances				£500	£650	£500
P PAYE/Hol.Cred				£3,767	£4,898	£3,767
Q Publicity						
R Miscellaneous expenses				£250	£325	£300
S Sets/models/props/dressing - construction				£150	£195	£250
T Special effects	1		£300	£300	£390	£300
U Special location facilities				£250	£325	£250
Total 'below the line' cost				**£16,693**	**£21,904**	**£15,537**
3 Indirect Costs:						
Y Finance & Legal				£250	£325	£250
Z Overheads				£300	£390	£300
Total indirect cost				**£550**	**£715**	**£550**
Total (1+2+3)				**£26,343**	**£34,449**	**£24,887**
Profit						**£9,562**

Appendix 2
Production Manager Job

Splitting a script into eighths and creating Script Breakdown/Production Board for budgeting and scheduling

Q. Why ia a page in a script split into eighths for budgeting and scheduling?

A. A scene on the page of a script (A4 paper size) to be filmed does not conveniently start at the top with its Scene Heading (slug line: INT. PARK - DAY) and end at the bottom of the page. Scenes are all different lengths, sometimes starting and ending in the middle of a page or going halfway into the next.

So - to gain an idea of how long it might take to film each scene bearing in mind 'time costs money' the method of eighths was conceived.

The A4 page is divided into 8 with each fractional eighth equalling 1 inch (2.54 centimetres). Using this method, the length of each scene equalling the amount of time to allocate to filming is now measurable as marked below in Figs. 1–3

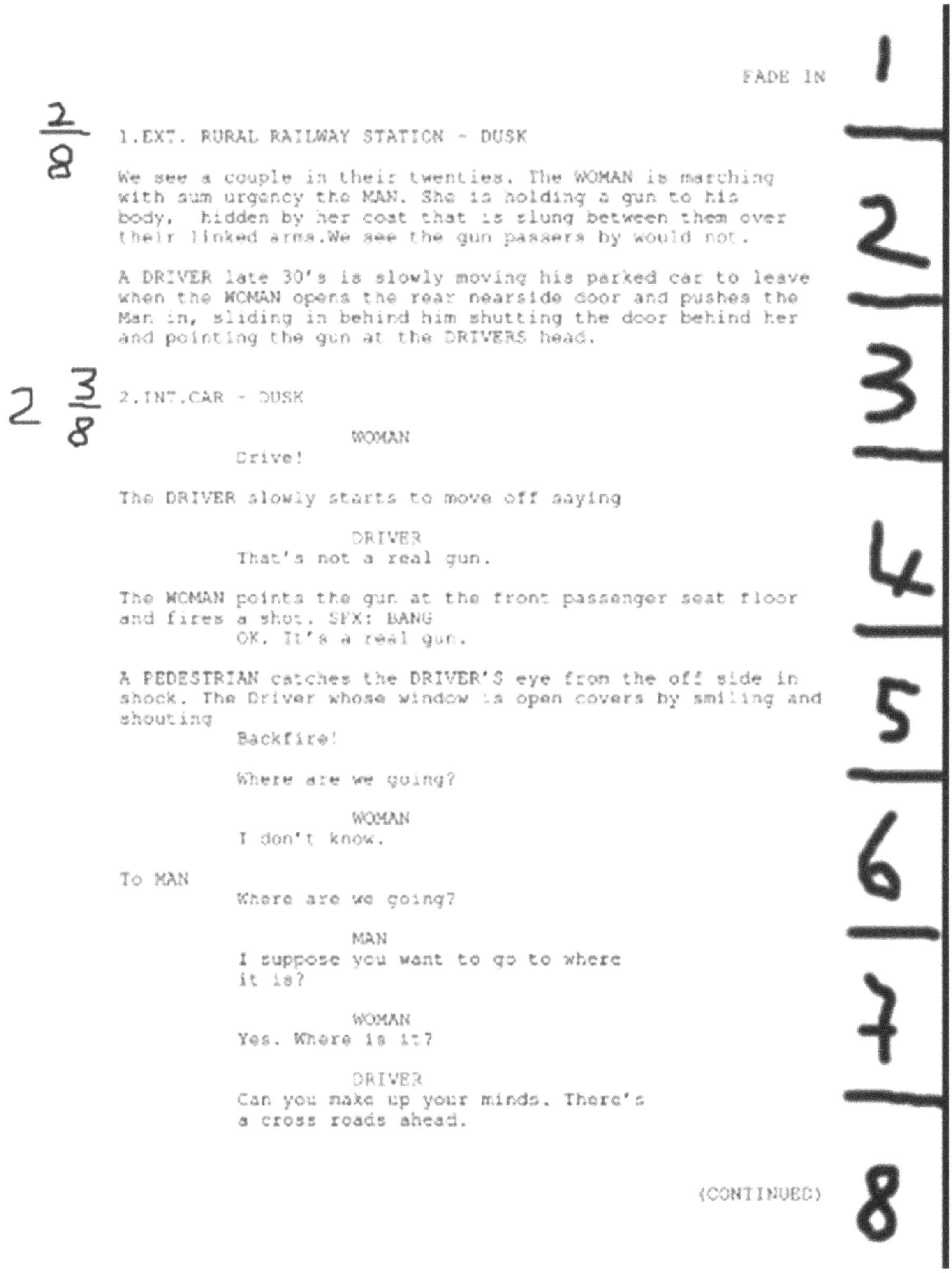

FADE IN

1

2/8

1.EXT. RURAL RAILWAY STATION - DUSK

2

We see a couple in their twenties. The WOMAN is marching
with sum urgency the MAN. She is holding a gun to his
body, hidden by her coat that is slung between them over
their linked arms.We see the gun passers by would not.

A DRIVER late 30's is slowly moving his parked car to leave
when the WOMAN opens the rear nearside door and pushes the
Man in, sliding in behind him shutting the door behind her
and pointing the gun at the DRIVERS head.

2   3/8   2.INT.CAR - DUSK

3

                         WOMAN
                    Drive!

The DRIVER slowly starts to move off saying

                         DRIVER
                    That's not a real gun.

4

The WOMAN points the gun at the front passenger seat floor
and fires a shot. SFX: BANG
                    OK. It's a real gun.

A PEDESTRIAN catches the DRIVER'S eye from the off side in
shock. The Driver whose window is open covers by smiling and
shouting

5

                    Backfire!

                    Where are we going?

                         WOMAN
                    I don't know.

6

To MAN

                    Where are we going?

                         MAN
                    I suppose you want to go to where
                    it is?

7

                         WOMAN
                    Yes. Where is it?

                         DRIVER
                    Can you make up your minds. There's
                    a cross roads ahead.

                                        (CONTINUED)

8

Fig. 1

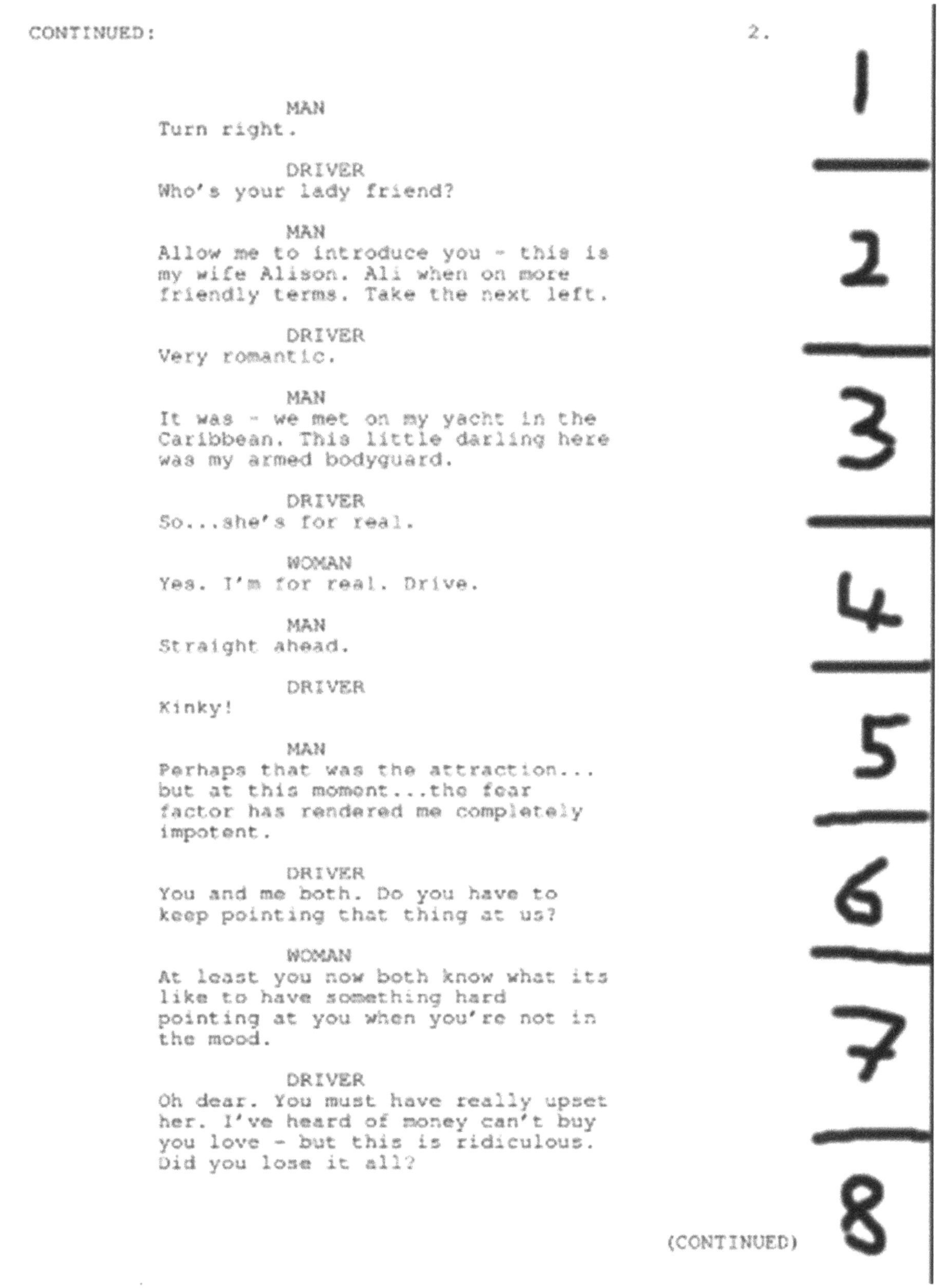

CONTINUED: 2.

                MAN
Turn right.

                DRIVER
Who's your lady friend?

                MAN
Allow me to introduce you - this is
my wife Alison. Ali when on more
friendly terms. Take the next left.

                DRIVER
Very romantic.

                MAN
It was - we met on my yacht in the
Caribbean. This little darling here
was my armed bodyguard.

                DRIVER
So...she's for real.

                WOMAN
Yes. I'm for real. Drive.

                MAN
Straight ahead.

                DRIVER
Kinky!

                MAN
Perhaps that was the attraction...
but at this moment...the fear
factor has rendered me completely
impotent.

                DRIVER
You and me both. Do you have to
keep pointing that thing at us?

                WOMAN
At least you now both know what its
like to have something hard
pointing at you when you're not in
the mood.

                DRIVER
Oh dear. You must have really upset
her. I've heard of money can't buy
you love - but this is ridiculous.
Did you lose it all?

                            (CONTINUED)

1

2

3

4

5

6

7

8

Fig. 2

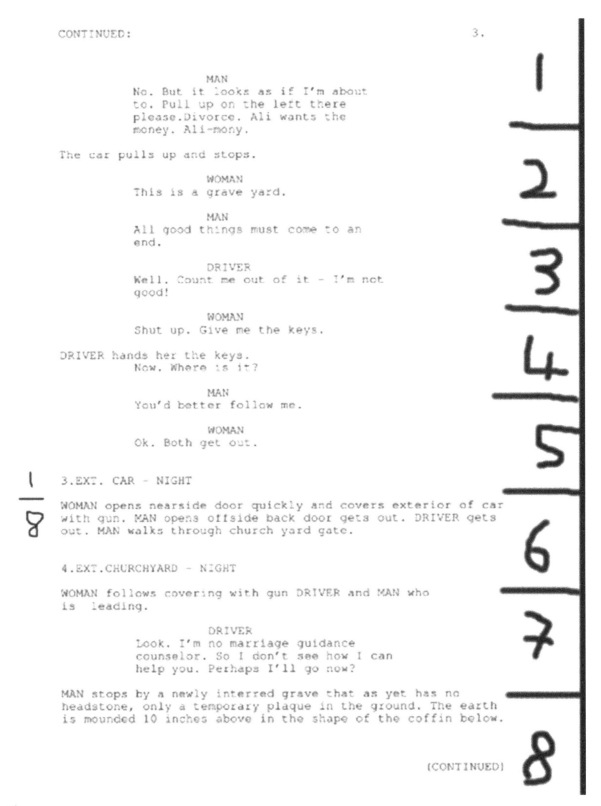

```
CONTINUED:                                                    3.

                            MAN
                No. But it looks as if I'm about
                to. Pull up on the left there
                please.Divorce. Ali wants the
                money. Ali-mony.

        The car pulls up and stops.

                            WOMAN
                This is a grave yard.

                            MAN
                All good things must come to an
                end.

                            DRIVER
                Well. Count me out of it - I'm not
                good!

                            WOMAN
                Shut up. Give me the keys.

        DRIVER hands her the keys.
                Now. Where is it?

                            MAN
                You'd better follow me.

                            WOMAN
                Ok. Both get out.


        3.EXT. CAR - NIGHT

        WOMAN opens nearside door quickly and covers exterior of car
        with gun. MAN opens offside back door gets out. DRIVER gets
        out. MAN walks through church yard gate.


        4.EXT.CHURCHYARD - NIGHT

        WOMAN follows covering with gun DRIVER and MAN who
        is  leading.

                            DRIVER
                Look. I'm no marriage guidance
                counselor. So I don't see how I can
                help you. Perhaps I'll go now?

        MAN stops by a newly interred grave that as yet has no
        headstone, only a temporary plaque in the ground. The earth
        is mounded 10 inches above in the shape of the coffin below.

                                                    (CONTINUED)
```

Fig. 3

Notice that Scene 2 Fig. 1 has been calculated as 6/8ths continuing to Fig. 2 as a complete page of 8/8ths to Fig. 3 calculated at 5/8ths by the end of the scene.

That makes a total of 19/8ths. With 8/8ths representing a page the scene is calculated as 2 × 8 = 2 pages plus 3/8ths. Written as above - 2. 3/8

Q. I'm still not sure what an eighth equals in shooting time?

A. Ah! You may as well ask 'how long is a piece of string?' Until you start shooting with crew and cast, a generous 'guestimate' will have had to have been made until after the first completed day of the shoot. A couple of days in you will then have a better idea of the speed the production is working at and be able to assess more accurately accordingly. The person who has the role of Production Manager will then be able to inform the Producer who holds the purse strings informing them of speedy or slow progress - if slow the Producer may start to panic! See documentary *Lost in La Mancha* (2002).

Script Breakdown 'Element' Colours

Element	Shape or color	Description
Cast	Red	Any speaking actor
Stunts	Orange	Any stunt that may require a stunt double, or stunt coordinator.
Extra (Silent bits)	Yellow	Any extra needed to perform specifically, but has no lines.
Extra (Atmosphere)	Green	Any extra or group of extras needed for the background.
Special Effects	Blue	Any special effect required.
Props	Purple	All objects important to the script, or used by an actor.
Vehicles/Animals	Pink	Any vehicles, and all animals, especially if it requires an animal trainer.
Sound Effects/Music	Brown	Sounds or music requiring specific use on set. Not sounds added in during post.
Wardrobe	Circle	Specific costumes needed for production, and also for continuity if a costume gets ripped up, or dirtied throughout the movie.
Make-up/Hair	Asterisk	Any make-up or hair attention needed. Common for scars and blood.
Special Equipment	Box	If a scene requires the use of more uncommon equipment, (e.g. crane, underwater camera, etc.).
Production Notes	Underline	For all other questions about how a scene will go, or confusion about how something happens.

Colours and attributes can vary - just make sure that your production sticks to the code selected and provides a legend/key on the title page.

Director note:

"The best education in film is to make one. I would advise any neophyte director to try to make a film by himself. A three-minute short will teach him a lot. I know that all the things I did at the beginning were, in microcosm, the things I'm doing now as a director and producer. **There are a lot of non-creative aspects to filmmaking which have to be overcome**, and you will experience them all when you make even the simplest film: business, organisation, budgets, taxes etc., etc." Stanley Kubrick

---

1. 2/8

INT.BEDSIT - NIGHT

We see a young wife ~~JANE HENSHAW~~ wearing surgical gloves mixing ~~anti-freeze~~ into a ~~bottle of Lambrini~~. She places the anti-freeze bottle in a cupboard.

On a ~~computer~~ she types
                    "I do not wish to be revived.
                    I want to die as I have planned
                    in peece."

She presses print. The ~~suicide note~~ emerges from the printer.She takes it and hides it along with the ~~surgical gloves~~ that she takes off once the note is in place.

Looking at her ~~watch~~ we see it reads 10.15pm. She puts up an ~~ironing board~~, turns some ~~music on~~ and starts to ~~iron~~ her nurses coat.

A key is heard in the door. It opens with ~~KIERAN~~ her husband struggling in from work drunk having come from the pub. He throws his coat off.

He goes and turns the music off.

Silence.

He struggles to sit at the table.

Then stares as JANE continues to iron while he grabs the bottle of Lambrini unscrews it and drinks. Then...

                         KIERAN
                  (coolly sneering at her)

Script Breakdown Sheet

For every scene in the script a separate **Script Breakdown Sheet** needs to be written up using the information colour coded above.

SCRIPT BREAKDOWN SHEET

Date 16/08/	Production Title Give Peace A Chance	Page 1 of 14
Director Mac Guffin	Production Company Mirror Up To Nature	Producer T.H.E Boss

1	Preparation for murder
Scene Number	Scene Description

CAST NOS	CAST/CHARACTER	INT/EXT	DAY/NIGHT	W/R	M/U
1 & 2	Jane Henshaw	INT	Night	Nurses Uniform/ Bra & Pants	for going to work
	Kieran Henshaw			Suit	pale - drunk -dead

STAND-INS	CROWD	LOCATION	ART DEPT/CONSTRUCTION	GRIPS
None	None	Bedsit - Studio 8 Elstree	Bedsit scenery	Jaqualine & Richard

CAMERA	LIGHTING	EXTRA EQUIPMENT	ACTION VEHICLES
C300 Mark 11	Full Kit	None	None

TRUCKS/TRAILERS	EXTRA CREW	PROPS/ANIMALS	SFX/WEAPONS
None	Full Crew	Sugical Gloves - Music Player - Bottle of Anti Freeze - Lambrini Bottle - Watch - Computer - Suicide Note	None

MISC - Substitute for real Anti Freeze & Lambrini !!!

N.B. For a very short film the logistical process of creating a **Production Board with Header Board and Day Strips** that would be put together using the information on **The Script Breakdown Sheets** is not necessary. However if you are able to have access to production software that enables you to put in the previous practical application that has been introduced to you here then all will be at your fingertips to complete. I recommend Celtx https://www.celtx.com/index.html where you are able to write your script and immediately integrate it with their production software. There are several others available (for preference) Studio Binder https://www.studiobinder.com/ being another that has industry approval.

Script 'page revision' colouring

(the following colours are now accepted as an industry standard for every time there is an amended scene)

1. White (unrevised)
2. Blue
3. Pink
4. Yellow
5. Green
6. Second Blue Revision
7. Second Pink Revision and so on…

The title page should list all the revision dates and colours in order. Each revised page should note the colour and date next to the page number at the top. For example: BLUE 15/09/2020 – p.56. Each revision needs to be done on a WHITE COPY so that copies on coloured paper copy clearly.

Appendix 3
Slate/Clapper Board

If you buy one for less than £20

a/ get some super glue and apply to the nuts here to stop them coming off.

Fig. 1

b/ use white gaffer tape to write information on that is then easily taken off and replaced. It's a good idea to wright in advance some regular numbers and letters that are likely to be used, <u>sticking them to the back of the board ready for use and re-use</u>.

c/ you may be tempted to download an app on your ipad or iphone to avoid using a physical board. Don't! It's small to read plus when your battery runs out you're helpless and…using the real article feels much more professional - you've arrived!

Etiquette

Be ready, standing in front of the camera with the board up and clapper sticks open. When you hear the director call 'Slate' or 'Mark it' or 'Board'.

Speak clearly: **"Scene Fifteen Charlie - Take Nine"** <u>clap the sticks</u> then **exit quietly** making sure you don't trip over cables - actors etc. Many a take has been ruined after the director has called Action by the person in your position clattering into something in the dark off set. Don't let that be you!

The Alphabet code words in Fig. 2 are used to call the Camera Positions

Alphabet	Code Word	Alphabet	Code Word
A	Alpha / Alfa	N	November
B	Bravo	O	Oscar
C	Charlie	P	Papa
D	Delta	Q	Quebec
E	Echo	R	Romeo
F	Foxtrot	S	Sierra
G	Golf	T	Tango
H	Hotel	U	Uniform
I	India	V	Victor
J	Juliet	W	Whiskey
K	Kilo	X	Xray
L	Lima	Y	Yankee
M	Mike	Z	Zulu

Fig. 2

As quoted previously from the slate marked up in Fig. 1 where it is written Scene 15.C. (Charlie) and following the camera position process **A-Z** explained in this book.

Roll = the digital card you are recording on (best to number them).

Scene = the number attributed in the shooting script plus Camera Position **A-Z** (you don't need to remark on the size of shot because the editor will see what it is CU - MCU etc)

Take = (could be 1 - 101) how many times the shot is re-shot in search of perfection.

Camera = can be either the camera used or the Director of Photography (DOP)

Day - Night = circle which it is.

Int - Ext = Interior - Exterior circle which it is.

Mos = Mute of Sound - circle if there is no sound and hold your fingers between the sticks to show the editor not to expect the sticks to be clapped.

Filter = can be named if used - in Fig.1 a Neutral Density Filter has been marked (ND)

Sync = Synchronisation. Circle if sound is being recorded.

Soft Sticks = if in front of an actor on a close up - don't hammer the sticks together loudly - do it softly calling out **'soft sticks'** so the editor knows not to expect to see a large spike in the waveform of the audio.

Tail Plate or End Board = if the slate was not called at the beginning of a shot for some reason then at the end of the shot with the sound and camera running hold the slate upside down - call the shot and clap it as you would have done at the start - then turn the slate the right way up so it can be read.

Avoid using the letters 'O' and 'I' when marking camera positions under scene heading - too easily confused with a Zero and One.

Appendix 4
Job Titles and Roles for an Indie/Guerrilla Short Film

Title	Role
Producer	Boss/Budget
Screenwriter	Story
Director	Interpreter
Production Manager	Manager 'Time is Money'
Script Supervisor	Continuity
Director of Photography (DOP)/ Camera Operator	Visuals
Sound Mixer/Supervisor	Sound
Boom Operator	Sound
Clapper Loader	Slate/Clapperboard
Gaffer	Lights
Gaffer Assistant/Best Boy	Lights
Grip	Camera supports
Actors	Talent
Costume & Make-Up	Look
Art Director	Set & Props

Of course, the role of Producer - Screenwriter - Director may all be you.

If so make sure you recruit a crew with at the very least an offer of food and expenses.

Engaging them to join in willingly in supporting your filmmaking adventure with enthusiasm, will be vital for your success.

Glossary

Filming terms and acronyms

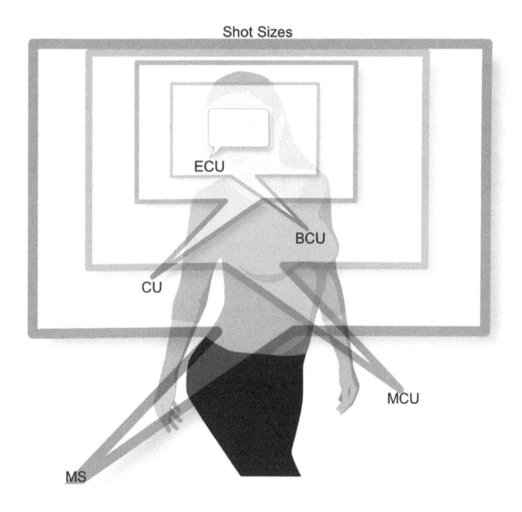

A

Above & Below The Line = when budgeting: **Above The Line** covers the cost of Producer - Director - Screenwriter - Lead Actors - DOP - and any other indispensable cost considered essential to a particular films success. **Below The Line** covers Crew and all other expenditure that may change but not jeopardise the films success.

Abby Singer Shot = second to last shot of the day. Named after Production Manager Abner E Singer. See also Martini & Jonesy Shots.

Action = actors and crew do their business.

Actor = female or male talent.

ADR = Automatic Dialogue Replacement. See Dubbing.

A- Roll = main footage. See B- Roll.

Alan Smithee = an Alan Smitthee directed film is one that the original director does not want their name associated with for many possible reasons. *Burn Hollywood Burn* (1997) is about that very subject that ironically ended up with its director wishing the same pseudonym to be attributable. Others include *Death of a Gunfighter (1969), Let's Get Harry* (1986) and *The Shrimp on the Barbie* (1990),

Arc Shot = dolly or track laid out in a curve or circle or such a freestyling camera movement.

Atmos = Room Tone - Location Sound - Wild Track. Sound at the location of a scene recorded for about a minute in silence for the atmosphere.

Auteur = 'a director who plagiarises their own work' it could be said. Over several of their films a familiar 'Trope' becomes attributable to them alone.

B

Below The Line = see Above The Line.

Best Boy = assistant electrician (male or female). See Gaffer.

BCU = Big Close Up.

Birds Eye = directly above.

B- Roll = cutaways and other alternative footage. See A -Roll.

Boom-pole = a pole held by the sound person that has a microphone at its end. See Fish-Pole.

Bokeh = see page 89

Buzz Track = see Atmos.

b.g = background.

C

Camera Right & Camera Left = screen (frame) right and screen (frame) left from viewer's point of view. **N.B. Actor note:** this is the opposite of Stage Right & Stage Left.

Contrapuntal sound = a contrast to what you see. Happy sounding music to an horrific event. Sad music to a happy event.

Crane = When you have a shot that starts extremely high and moves to a lower position or vice versa. Often used for overhead and establishing shots.

Crew = all the technicians involved in a shoot.

Cheat = see pages 69, 70

Cinematographer = see pages 77–79

Continuity = see page 58

Contingency Plan = a backup plan if...see Murphy's Law.

Coverage = see pages 55–57

CU = Close Up.

Cut = crew and actors stop filming.

Cutaway = a Close Up shot or wide Shot looking at something away from the matching action sequence of shots. Often needed as a saviour shot that can be inserted into a sequence if there is a continuity error. See page 63

D

Diffuser (paper) Gel = is not tracing paper! It looks like it but if that were used the fire brigade would be needed. Diffuser Gel is used for softening your lighting while not burning under intense heat of an 800 watt Red Head lamp.

Diegetic sound = actual sound from inside the scene as it is happening.

Dolly = When you move the entire camera forwards and backwards along a track.

Dolly Zoom = A technique where the camera moves closer or further from the subject while simultaneously adjusting the zoom angle to keep the subject the same size in the frame. See page 64

DOP = Director Of Photography - see Cinematographer

Dubbing = see ADR.

Dutch Angle/German Angle/Canted Angle = a slanted shot.

E

ECU = Extreme Close Up.

EL = Eye Level.

Establishing Shot = what it says - letting your audience know the location.

EXT = exterior.

F

fav = favouring.

f.g = foreground.

FS = **Full Shot** head to toe of a character with little else in view.

Film Noir = a French phrase literally meaning "black film" that developed in the early 40s; refers to a genre of mostly black/white films that blossomed in the post-war era in American cinema, with bleak subject matter and a sombre, downbeat tone; the plot (often a quest), low-key lighting (harsh shadows and **chiaroscuro**) often in night scenes, camera angles (often **canted** or high angle shots), the setting (the gloomy underworld of crime and corruption), iconography (guns, urban settings), characters (disillusioned, jaded), and other elements (**voice-overs** and **flashbacks**) combined to present a dark atmosphere of pessimism, tension, cynicism, or oppression. Film noirs, often crime films, were usually set in grim and seedy cities, with characters including criminals, **anti-heroes**, private detectives, and duplicitous *femme fatales*.[33]

Fish-pole = see Boom-pole

Foley = see pages 114–115

Fourth Wall = the one the audience 'gazes' through without being 'gazed' back at by the characters in the scene unless intentionally. See page 23

G

Gaffer Tape = it's not Duct Tape! Although it looks the same it is much kinder to property, not leaving a sticky residue that hosts at a location would not appreciate.

Gaffer = head electrician. See Best Boy.

Gel = Lighting gel is a flexible polycarbonate or polyester material (similar to acetate). The most frequently needed is a daylight blue gel attached in front of film lights to match the colour temperature of outside daylight.

---

[33] https://www.filmsite.org/filmterms1.html

Gobo = a cut-out shape placed in front of a light source to manipulate the shape of light cast over a space or object.

Guerrilla film = low budget - how most start a venture in the film industry - for love not money! See Indie filmmaking.

Grip = member of the crew who sets up Sticks - Tracking - Scaffolding - Scenery and heavy props etc.

H

HA = High Angle.

Handheld = The camera is held by the operator without a stabilizer.

Health & Safety = see Risk Assessment.

High Key Lighting = a bright lighting scheme appropriate for comedies.

I

Indie Filmmaking = Independent, often low budget. See Guerrilla.

INT = interior.

J

Jonesy Shot = First shot of the day. In 2014 Sarah Jones, assistant camera woman on a never to be completed film *Midnight Rider* was setting up the first shot on a railway bridge in Georgia USA when a freight train travelling at high speed left her no time to clear. Today calling this first shot in tribute to her is a reminder for all concerned to make sure that risk assessments have been fully carried out. The producer of the film was sentenced to 10 years in 2015. Here is a news report with some footage of the fatal incident.

https://youtu.be/-7K4s2xRO9Q

Make sure you carry out Risk Assessments - form appendix page 295 See also Martini & Abby Shots.

K

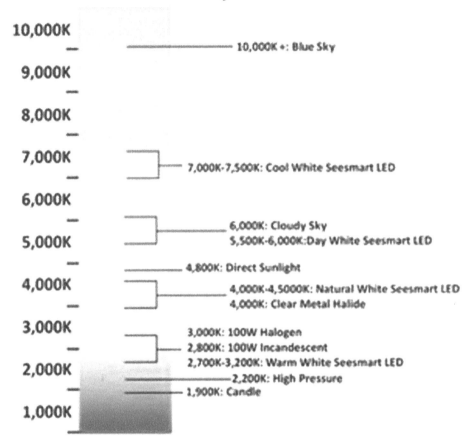

Kelvin Color Temperature Scale

10,000K

10,000K +: Blue Sky

9,000K

8,000K

7,000K

7,000K-7,500K: Cool White Seesmart LED

6,000K

6,000K: Cloudy Sky

5,000K

5,500K-6,000K:Day White Seesmart LED

4,800K: Direct Sunlight

4,000K

4,000K-4,5000K: Natural White Seesmart LED

4,000K: Clear Metal Halide

3,000K

3,000K: 100W Halogen

2,800K: 100W Incandescent

2,700K-3,200K: Warm White Seesmart LED

2,000K

2,200K: High Pressure

1,900K: Candle

1,000K

L

LA = Low Angle.

LED Lights = Light-emitting diode - see pages 80–83

Legs = Tripod - Sticks.

Location Sound = see Atmos.

Low Key Lighting = under or dimly lit atmosphere for horror thriller or film noir genres.

LS = Long Shot.

M

MacGuffin = an object, event, or character in a film or story that serves to set and keep the plot in motion despite usually lacking intrinsic importance.

Martini Shot = the last shot of the day. See also Abby & Jonesy Shots.

Master Shot = showing characters and objects geographically in a scene from the beginning to the end of it.

MCU = Medium Close Up.

MLS = Medium Long Shot.

MS = Mid Shot.

Murphy's Law = 'anything that can go wrong will go wrong'. Be prepared with a contingency plan!

Mise-en-scène = everything seen in the frame - actors - scenery etc.

N

Non-diegetic sound = mood music - narration - sound effects - and any other sound that is added to what is in the scene.

O

O.S = Out of Shot.

OTS = Over The Shoulder Shot.

P

Pan = Horizontal camera movement left to right.

Pedestal = When the camera is moved vertically up or down (without tilting).

POV = Point of View. Subjective Camera Angle.

Pull focus = when the focus changes from one subject to another in the same shot. See page 91

R

Rack focus = Pull focus.

Reaction Shot = see page 67

Recce = (pro: Recky) Reconnaissance: assessing suitable locations ahead of filming.

Risk assessment = see Jonesy Shot and Risk assessment form appendix 295

Room Tone = see Atmos.

Rule of Thirds = see page 58

S

Scene = what happens start to finish at a location in continuous time often comprising of various shots of a character or characters that starts with filming the Master Shot.

Sequence = a sequence comprises of several scenes put together showing the emotional journey of the story.

SFX = Special Effects.

Shot = what is recorded from 'Action' to 'Cut'.

Shutter Speed/Shutter Angle = the way to control the exposure time. It is not the same as the Frame Rate which represents how many frames are exposed per second as in Fig. 1 below that is reading 24 Frames per second (24 fps), the recognised film rate.

1																							24

Fig. 1

Within **each of those frames** above we have the way you control the exposure time represented as either a Shutter Speed or Shutter Angle shown below in Fig. 2

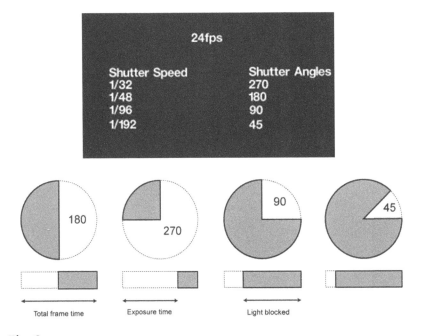

Fig. 2

With Cinema Cameras the shutter speed is given as degrees (Angles). Some cameras offer you a choice of both. Simply know that the slower the shutter speed you gain more light longer exposure time that may show a more blurred image. Thus, the rule of thumb for most standard shoots is a setting of either 180 degrees or 1/48th of a second (1/50th at 25 fps). However, if you were shooting something like a motor race to avoid a blurred image you would shoot at as high a shutter speed or low angle as the reduced amount of light through the lens would allow. **N.B.** an example of your knowledge here could be used in an either-or scenario: confetti cascading over a happy couple filmed with a low Shutter Angle (high Shutter Speed) would allow for a crystal-clear slow-motion cascade of confetti. A high Shutter Angle in slow motion would be blurred. The aesthetic choice is yours!

Static camera = what it says - not moving.

Steadicam = When the camera is stabilized using a special rig onto the body of a specialized operator. See pages 64–65

Spike The Lens = unintentionally glance into the camera breaking the fourth wall.

Sticks = Tripod - Legs.

Subjective Camera Angle = see POV

Synching or Syncing = putting sound and vision together.

T

Take = with the camera and sound recording, spoken by the Clapper Loader before each shot 'take one' followed by the director calling 'Action'. The number of each successive **take is called incrementally 2, 3, 4, 5...** until the director is satisfied and ready to move onto the next setup.

Tilt = vertical camera movement up and down.

Tracking/Truck = The same as dollying, only you are moving the entire camera from left to right instead of forward and backward.

Trope = a dominant or recurring idea in an artistic work.

Tripod = Legs or Sticks to hold camera.

2-S = Two Shot.

V

V.O = Voice Over.

W

Wild Track = see Atmos.

WS = Wide Shot.

Wrap = "A Wrap" or "It's A Wrap" end of filming.

Wrap for the Day = end of filming for the day.

X

XCU = see ECU.

XLR Cable = balanced male and female audio connector cable.

Z

Zoom = When you zoom in or out of a subject. See page 64

Useful Websites

General interest

BBC (British Broadcasting Company) Writers Room - TV writing tips
https://www.bbc.co.uk/writersroom/

BBC Academy (British Broadcasting Company) - TV production tips
https://www.bbc.co.uk/academy/en

BFI (British Film Institute) UK's lead organisation for film, television and the moving image.
https://www.bfi.org.uk/

Movie & TV screenplays to view
http://www.script-o-rama.com/

Glossary plus many interesting facts about filmmaking
https://www.filmsite.org/filmterms1.html

The Writers Store - online industry books
https://www.writersstore.com/storyboard-quick/

Den of Geek - where to go to become a grown up 'movie geek'
https://www.denofgeek.com/uk/movies

Internet Movie Data Base
https://www.imdb.com/

Instutute of Videography
www.iov.co.uk

Movie Mistakes
https://www.moviemistakes.com/

Public Domain films on YouTube
https://www.youtube.com/results?search_query=public+domain+films+uk

Producers' Alliance for Cinema and Television
http://www.pact.co.uk/

Video Maker - cameras - editing - latest technology updates
https://www.videomaker.com/

Tutorials - workshops - advice

Both Sides of the Movie camera – this books website
www.bothsidesofthemoviecamera.film

Shooting People - Shooting People connects you with thousands of filmmakers,
actors, crew, technologists and industry to get films made and seen.
https://shootingpeople.org/

Film Directing Tips
http://filmdirectingtips.com/archives/157

Online Master Classes with Oscar winning greats
https://www.masterclass.com/

Actors Centre - training for actors 'when resting'
https://www.actorscentre.co.uk/

Screenskills - job roles and advice for getting into the industry
https://www.screenskills.com/

On Line Video co pilot - After Effect Tutorials & Plugins
https://www.videocopilot.net/

Online Linkedin Learning Tutorials - premiere pro - after effects et al.
https://www.linkedin.com/learning/topics/creative

Inside The Actors Studio - James Lipton - famous actors discuss their method
https://www.bravotv.com/inside-the-actors-studio

Skillshare – film online tutorials
https://www.skillshare.com/

Wolfcrow online film tutorials
https://wolfcrow.com/

Software

Adobe Creative Cloud - all in one editing integration software
https://www.adobe.com/uk/creativecloud.

Avid the leading first non-linear digital editing system all others are based on
https://www.avid.com/

Maya 3D computer animation & effects
https://www.autodesk.com/products/maya/overview

DeVinci Resolve colour grading software
https://www.blackmagicdesign.com/products/davinciresolve/

Unions

Actors Union
https://www.equity.org.uk/home

Broadcasting, Entertainment, Communications and Theatre Union
https://www.bectu.org.uk/home

Pre Production software

Set Hero - production scheduling software
https://setheroapp.com/blog/film-script-schedule-revision-colors/

Movie Magic
https://www.ep.com/home/managing-production/movie-magic-scheduling/

Storyboad Creator - the original industry storyboard software
https://www.storyboardthat.com/storyboard-creator

Storyboard Quick - software
https://www.powerproduction.com/index.php

Studio Binder - all production software
https://www.studiobinder.com/shot-list-storyboard/

Celtx - Screenwriting & full Production Software
https://www.celtx.com/index.html

Final Draft the original Screenwriting sofware
https://store.finaldraft.com

Film Contracts & Agreements
https://www.filmdaily.tv/template/film-contracts-and-agreements-protect-your-film

Free pre-production templates to download
http://www.dependentfilms.net/files.html

Copyright

Public Domain film check advice
https://www.buyoutfootage.com/pages/faq_publicdomain.php

Copyright user advice
https://www.copyrightuser.org/create/creators-discuss/filmmaker/

ound Recording Copyright
tps://www.gov.uk/government/publications/copyright-in-sound-recordings

PPL Phonographic Performance Limited - Music Licensing Company
https://www.ppluk.com/about-us/

Wikimedia Commons - free images as long as the author's source is credited
https://commons.wikimedia.org

Film Festivals

Urban Black Film Festival
https://www.britishurbanfilmfestival.co.uk/

Independent Films UK based plus workshops
https://www.raindance.org/

UK Film Festivals
https://www.ukfilmfestival.com/

Sundance - organization that actively advances the work of independent
storytellers in film
www.sundance.org

Books

Cook.K. et al (2019) Video Skills Digital Technical Filmmaking Competences.
Institute of Videography

Tucker. P (2019) Secrets of Screen Acting. Routledge

Marshall. D. P (2019) Making Magic Happen. Directing. Michael Wiese Books

Field.S. (2016) Screenwriting. Ebury Press

Podcasts

BFI network
https://network.bfi.org.uk/news-and-features/podcasts

Indie Wire - link to film podcasts
https://www.indiewire.com/2017/04/best-film-podcasts-1201804799/

Acknowledgements

DVD's

Packaging Medium Rare Entertainment *Charade*

Republic Entertainment Inc and Republic Pictures *It's A Wonderful Life*

Classic Entertainment *Farewell To Arms*

Images

wikimedia commons images - *Carbon arc studio spotlight - Shutter Speed Shutter Angle - Scripting Element Colours*
www.eneltec-led.com *Kelvin Scale*

Storyboard by Charles Ratteray for Joss Whedon's "Buffy the Vampire Slayer" Filmmakeriq *Psycho Storyboard* Photo courtesy of Filmmakeriq *www.graphicadi.com - colour grading picture*

Jack Foley *in the editing studio. Courtesy of Jack Foley* YouTube upload shot grabs - *Psycho - Schindler's List - Intolerance - Persona - Casablanca - Kings Speech - The Cabinet of Dr.Caligari- Nosferatu - Sunrise*

Every effort has been made to credit photographs and illustrations. Should there have been any omissions or errors please accept the publisher's apologies who will be pleased to make the appropriate correction for future editions.

Quick Response (QR codes):

Copyright Disclaimer under section 107 of Copyright Act 1976, allowance is made for "fair use" for purposes such as criticism, comment, news reporting, teaching, scholarship, and research. Fair use permitted by copyright statute that might otherwise be infringing. Non-profit, educational or personal use tips the balance in favour of fair use.

About the Author

Anthony Barnett MA is a former National Theatre actor, director, writer, filmmaker, lecturer in Film/TV and Performing Arts, Master Member of the Institute of Videography, known for his master classes at The Actors' Centres (London/Manchester), Royal Central School of Speech and Drama, colleges and universities. Early in his career, Anthony heard a technician remark about his film performance on set the humiliating sentence "very good for a stage performance"! *Both Sides of the Movie Camera* guides actors how *not* to hear the same remark and directors on how to get screen performances and direct a winning short film - a calling card into the industry.

Make good use of the books dedicated website
www.bothsidesofthemoviecamera.film

for book resources, tutorials, interviews and examples.

"The day we know it all, should be the day only
a Medium can get in touch with us".

Thanks to the Editor

I thank Anthony Manning (CEO of Institute of Videography) for his extraordinary patience in editing away my stray apostrophe's (oh dear, there one goes again!), spelling, incomprehensible sentences (with me trying to defend them with "it's my style"): thus, he has survived, this author's literary delusions, with his always benevolent appreciation of Both Sides of the Movie Camera's intention, that of succouring the neophyte actor and director in their creative hour of need.

Index

Lightning Source UK Ltd.
Milton Keynes UK
UKHW051321260522
403553UK00004B/28